)NTENTS

....

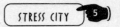

CHAPTER 1

INTRODUCTION

This is a book on a subject which is sometimes difficult for people to notice in themselves. If you have an irritable friend, or one with PMS (premenstrual syndrome), the first people to suffer may be the ones who are getting their heads bitten off, not the stressed out mate doing the biting. Others are often aware of a problem and of someone behaving irrationally or differently from normal, and may even need to point it out to the sufferer before they become fully aware of their behaviour.

The difference between someone who is emotionally well, and someone who isn't can be strikingly obvious! Problems which you could cope with easily when you are happy and well, can feel like disasters when times are tough, as though life's out to get you.

Life's a gas

If nothing interesting, unusual or exciting ever happened life would be so dull and boring. If the sun shone on us and our lives every day, and we only had good times and better times, we would be emotionally flat and empty. Whilst the animal kingdom may feel a variety of basic emotions, human beings are set apart by an ability to think, problem solve, and have emotional responses ranging from black despair to total joy.

Our entire lives are spent problem solving …

and making decisions about the best way forward for us.

No matter how you try and avoid it, stress will always be part of your life. Choices must be made, goals reached, obstacles overcome and delays put up with. Everyone has pressures and most of us develop ways of coping with them. Some days we breeze through life like a dream and other days turn into nightmares and you wonder why you bothered to get out of bed. You know, those real bad hair days, the ones where everything from an alarm clock which fails to go off makes you late/you can't get in the bathroom/haven't time for breakfast/miss the bus/realise your money has been left at home/turn back and walk into a lamp-post type — Stress City days!

What is Stress?

A nice vague definition is needed here, because stress means different things to different people, and everyone has their own way of reacting, but really it's how your mind and body responds to any mental or physical demand made on it. Stress is a general term used to describe any pressure you are under and the ways in which you deal with it. Everyone meets stress during their lifetime, whether it's a major thing like someone close dying, to a not so major thing, like what you're going to wear to a birthday party.

The time I felt stressed was when I was bullied at school at the start of the year. I never told anyone about it and had to cope on my own.

(14-YEAR-OLD GIRL)

We're given too much homework to do and not enough time to do it in. This usually happens weekends and I sometimes feel it's only ever happening to me!

(15-YEAR-OLD BOY)

'Things that stress me out': 14–17 year olds

- family
- learning to drive
- lack of money
- too much work
- my size
- being late
- noise
- weather
- pollution
- nagging parents
- dad's dancing
- stupid people
- illness
- friends
- work deadlines
- my spots
- traffic jams
- my football injury

- being dumped by my girlfriend after my exams

I was most stressed out when I had exams at school and one outside of school, playing the piano. I didn't have time to do my homework as I had to go home and cook tea, then I had to go to cadets where I was in charge of some people.
(14-YEAR-OLD GIRL)

The thing that stressed me out the most was when my nan died. We were really close to each other.
(14-YEAR-OLD BOY)

How your body reacts

The weird thing is that you can respond in the same way to loads of different stressful things. If you feel threatened, or try a bungee jump, or fall into an icy cold stream, or see something which scares you, you will react with a response that's been with you since you were born. It works something like this:

You feel threatened Ⅲ➡ Stress response triggered Ⅲ➡ Stress response switched off Ⅲ➡ Physical changes in the body to help Ⅲ➡ Escape behaviour

This innate, or inborn response is there to help you survive and you may have heard it called the fight or flight response. So exactly what happens to your body when this response takes over?

The Fight or Flight Response

To deal with any emergency or seen threat you need energy, quick!

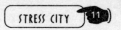

Some of the things that happen are:

- **senses become more acute**
- **skin sweats to cool body**
- **increased breathing rate, racing heartbeat**
- **digestion shuts down**
- **rise in blood pressure**
- **non-essential activity stops**
- **saliva dries up**
- **release of body's natural painkillers**
- **release of sugar to provide quick energy**
- **muscles tense ready for action**
- **blood thickens**

So ...

- your liver releases sugar, and hormones (the body's natural chemicals) converting fats and proteins in the body to sugar. This helps to fuel your muscles ready for action, giving them a boost of adrenaline if you have to fight or flee!

- your metabolism increases. In other words, your heart beats faster (you may even hear it thumping), your blood pressure rises and your breathing rate increases to pump more blood to the muscles and the lungs.

- anything not essential stops to allow blood to be delivered else-where. You may also feel you need the loo - get that non-essential waist out of the way!

- your spit (saliva) dries up. This is to increase the size of the air passages to the lungs — more oxygen means more fuel. This is often noticed by people who have to get up on stage or say something in front of others. When you try to smile, there's no spit left in your mouth, so your top lip sticks to your teeth and you end up smiling like some kind of maniac!

- the body's natural pain killers (called endorphins) are produced and blood vessels on the surface of the skin constrict. This means that if you are injured, you feel less pain and there's less blood from minor injuries. If ever you've been hurt playing sport, you'll know all about this. Some rugby and football players have been known to play on all match with broken bits and not realise they're hurt until after they've stopped playing because the endorphins produce a 'high' feeling which masks the pain.

- skin changes. It may pale and sweat or feel as though it's crawling. Sweating provides increased cooling for the muscles and body.

- the bloodstream is flooded with adrenaline to allow all this to happen.

Never-ending stress

These bodily responses are useful for fast action in emergencies. If you deal with the threat quickly and it goes away, then your body goes back to normal after a few minutes or hours. It is not unusual to feel tired or headachy after extreme excitement as your body's chemicals settle down. There are problems though, when the stress doesn't go away. Our bodies were not designed to handle physical and mental stress that continues hour after hour or day after day.

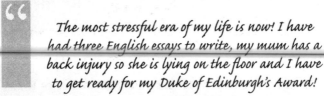

The most stressful era of my life is now! I have had three English essays to write, my mum has a back injury so she is lying on the floor and I have to get ready for my Duke of Edinburgh's Award!

(15-YEAR-OLD GIRL)

If stresses and concerns carry on and on, like someone close being

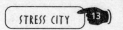

very ill, working towards exams, or your parents' separation, then you will be likely to experience three physical changes:

- **alarm**
- **resistance**
- **exhaustion**

These work something like this:

1 You feel threatened *which*

2 Triggers the stress response

3 Leads to exhaustion

4 Physical changes occur in the body to help

5 Prolonged stress response

6 Escape — fight or run away

7 Stressed state continues

8 Fight or flight doesn't work

Because the stress response never gives the body a chance to rest then quite a few things could happen. Stress reactions use up a lot of your body's physical resources and this means your body can't devote the same amount of effort to fighting off illness and dis-

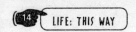

ease. You'll be more likely to catch colds and 'flu and other stress-related illnesses. Headaches and feeling irritable are common symptoms of stress, as are sleep and skin problems. Skin problems could range from that big spot which erupts on the end of your nose the morning of an important day when you want to look your best, to eczema, psoriasis, dry or oily skin, changes in normal skin colour, to more spots than you ever thought possible. Even though you wash, eat well and try to get enough sleep, those skin changes just don't seem to be improving.

Often people don't recognise that they are under stress because they don't relate the way they're feeling to other problems in their life and can't make comparisons to what are normal emotions, and what aren't. In the short term stress can cause symptoms like:

- **nail-biting**
- **needing the loo (a lot!)**
- **sweating or shaking**
- **having 'butterflies' in the stomach**
- **nervous laughter**
- **talking a lot**
- **not communicating as normal**
- **headaches**
- **feeling sick**
- **dry mouth**
- **getting angry over little things**

If the stress is more long-term then you could get symptoms like:

- **muscle tension (especially across the shoulders and the neck)**
- **asthma**
- **skin rashes**
- **stomach problems**
- **backache**
- **sleeplessness**
- **blood pressure changes**
- **poor concentration**
- **fatigue**
- **depression**
- **worsening PMS**
- **heart palpitations**
- **eczema**
- **breathing difficulties**

If you have a friend who may start to complain a lot about all sorts of aches and pains, some vague, some more obvious (like those spots) you could ask yourself what else may be going on in their lives. Maybe they have lots of grief going on, and in some way are trying to say 'Hey, notice me, I'm not well, I can't cope'. Can you help them? Can you ask questions and find out what is really worrying them, help them to recognise they may have a problem they can't handle alone, and see what can be done next to sort things out?

How to chill

There are lots of ways to cope with the stress that life throws at you. Many of these you'll have already discovered for yourself through experience, and this book will suggest many others which could work for you

What this book hopes to do is to take you through some of the things that give you stress and to suggest a few ways of coping with these hassles. Sometimes recognising that you or a friend are stressed is the first step towards dealing with it. Knowing that you're not alone and that there are others feeling the same way can also be reassuring!

> *Friends really stress me out when they accuse me of doing things that I haven't. They ignore me and talk about me behind my back. It makes me feel depressed when they do this and it makes me feel small and left out.*
>
> (14-YEAR-OLD GIRL)

Stress Scale

Why not have a go at the stress scale below. Assess how you feel at the end of the day. Do this for one week, then add up your seven scores and see how stressed you think you are.

1	2	3	4	5	6	7	8	9	10
'I feel great'				'I feel ok'				'I feel awful'	

7–29: You're not under a vast amount of stress, or you're coping with it really well!

30–49: You consider yourself to be under a fair amount of stress. Take time out to relax a little more and make some time for you.

50–70: This score shows you consider yourself to be under a lot of pressure. Talk to someone close about how you're feeling. Work out ways of reducing your stress. If this level of stress were to continue over the next year you may find yourself more prone to stress-related illnesses. Chill out!

So have a read through 'Stress City'. You may recognise some of the same problems that you're having, or perhaps a friend's going through a rough patch. There are lots of things that can stress you out, but there are also ways to reduce your stress. Find the right balance and life will be a breeze! (Sometimes!)

CHAPTER 2

ALL STRESSED UP

 I felt stressed when my brother kept bullying me when I was trying to do my coursework for English. I was so angry I had headaches!
(14-YEAR-OLD BOY)

Stress for ever and a day

We know that we'll go through stresses of varying degrees at some time in our lives. So if this is true, you may be wondering why everyone in the world isn't struck down by stress related illnesses. The extreme physical and mental pressures of long term stress may leave your body vulnerable to some of the following:

- **lowered resistance to germs and viruses**
- **weight loss**
- **jumpy nerves/ irritability**
- **sleeplessness**
- **reduced resistance to pain**
- **feeling sick**
- **more risk of heart disease**
- **high blood pressure**
- **loss of concentration**
- **exhaustion**
- **more risk of diabetes**
- **tummy disorders**
- **migraines and backache**
- **sweat more**

Why don't we all get these symptoms? The simple answer to that is we are all different. As individuals we all have different personalities and have had different lives which have shaped those personalities. Some of us cope better than others in times of crisis, but the way we deal with stress can vary over the years. You may well find that at one point in your life you cope very well with all the rubbish that life throws at you. At another it may take just one tiny little thing to reduce you to a gibbering wreck! Sometimes stress just creeps up on you, little problems just seem to snowball, you think you are coping with each one as it comes along, but the total amount of the grief you are getting is actually starting to get you down. In this situation you may often miss the early symptoms, and put them down to a virus, lack of sleep, part of growing up and out.

The thing that stresses me out most is not having enough money and girls messing about with my emotions.

(15-YEAR-OLD BOY)

I was stressed when I had my belly button pierced. All I felt was worry and I was frightened. But I really wanted it done.

(15-YEAR-OLD GIRL)

Type A or Type B: which are you?

It has been suggested that there are certain personality types that cope with stress better than others. Type A people are more likely to get stress-related illnesses than Type B. Their expectations and criticisms of themselves and others are too harsh to be realistic. They may in fact have low self esteem and be continually trying to improve, not recognising that we are only human. And humans ain't perfect! Type B people are more relaxed and reasonable about themselves and others.

So which one best describes you? Circle each of the numbers below if you feel you identify with the statement, don't take too long and think too hard, as we're all different in different situations, just go for the main type as you read through:

TYPE A

1 Intense/ambitious but vague about aims
2 Quick and alert
3 Easily irritated
4 Intolerant and impatient with others
5 Competitive at work /school
6 Find it hard to work at slow pace
7 Can't pass on jobs to others/ feels can do the job better
8 Perfectionist

intense?
easily irritated?
impatient?
Intolerant?

TYPE B

1 More relaxed
2 Works just as hard but can chill
3 Tries not to worry about future
4 Able to switch off when away
5 Able to pass on jobs without feeling need to supervise
6 Prioritises things to be done
7 Does the best they can
8 Accepts that other people are different

Relaxed? Chilled? Able to switch off? Can delegate?

It's got to be a Type B for me

How many did you recognise as being your type? More As or Bs?

All is not lost if you identify more with the Type A personality than Type B: many people are a mixture of both and find they can unwind when they need to at home, and work flat out at their jobs or at school. Both personality types get where they want to go, Type Bs seem to manage it without creating a lot of hassle for themselves.

If you know that you are definitely a Type A, then you may need to think about your stress levels. Try to take on some of the Type Bs ways of looking at life. Approach everyday stresses with a positive 'I can' attitude rather than a negative 'I can't' mentality. Think about the way you manage your time; rather than mess about at a loose end, take an active step towards relaxing or achieving small jobs or goals. Try to trust other people to do things you ask of them, but don't expect perfection —everyone is human and no one else will do something identically to the way you might do it. If you have trouble concentrating, then set yourself a time limit, and do that one thing for the fifteen minutes or whatever you give yourself. after you have achieved that target, give yourself a reward. It doesn't have to be food! Type Bs know they can't change the past, that they did their best in the given circumstances of a particular situation. Whilst they might learn from the experience, they don't spend hours fretting over what might have been. They look forward, not back, you could try the same.

Being in Control

> *The most stressful thing for me is when my brother gets to my mum and makes her cry. I feel so frustrated because I can't do anything about it.*
> (14-YEAR-OLD BOY)

Control is also an important issue in dealing with your stress. If you feel that you are in control of your life and can actively do something to change it, then you'll feel far less stress than someone who feels they have no control at all. This is called your locus of control and you can either have an internal or external one! Internalisers (let's call them ITs) can deal with stress much more positively than Externalisers (let's call them ETs). This could also explain why people who experience the same amount of stress deal with it (and cope with it) differently.

Tick the any of the following three statements for each personality which you feel applies to you:

Internalisers believe:

• **they can do something about their situations;**

• **in being active in shaping their lives;**

• **inside influences can overcome any problem**

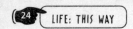
Internalisers have a positive outlook on life, they are the type of people who say 'I can...'

Externalisers believe:

- **they can't do anything to change their situation;**
- **they are helpless;**
- **outside influences are shaping what is happening**
  and can't be controlled.

Externalisers are more likely to have a negative outlook, you hear them saying 'I can't...'

Did you tick more statements from one of the lists? Are you more usually an IT 'I can' or an ET 'I can't' type of person? Which attitude do you think would cope more easily with everyday problems? Problem solving and dealing with stresses can be heavily influenced by the way you look at life — when you see a glass of water, do you see it as half-full (as an IT would) or a half-empty (as an ET might)? Do you have an internal or external locus of control? It's quite easy to pick out which of your friends are which. Listen to things they say after a test at school. ETs will blame other influences, make excuses and say things like:

ITs, on the other hand, will realise that they themselves bear responsibility for their work and say things like:

Sound familiar? You may have even said them yourself! ITs will learn something from the experience, and be more likely to change their approach to preparing next time. They are more likely to take responsibility for themselves and say statements including the word 'I'. ETs will use 'He/she/they' as they try to absolve themselves of responsibility and blame anything and everyone else for their stress, without first looking at their own actions. ITs understand what it takes to succeed and know what can be done. ETs have to stop making excuses/finding fault/blaming others and look at themselves for the solution.

Again, there is a possibility that at different times in your life you could swap over from one to the other. In certain situations you may feel well in control of what's going on, at other times you may feel as though it's all out of your hands.

> I get stressed out when I forget to do a big homework and then I haven't got enough time to do it properly. I also feel stressed if mum's unhappy because she goes around the house huffing, making me feel low. When mum's unhappy I usually have problems at school. I get picked on sometimes. I can't talk to mum about it otherwise she'd get worked up.
>
> (14-YEAR-OLD GIRL)

Downward spiral

Have you ever found yourself in a kind of downward spiral of despair, or feel like you are wading through treacle. You seem to have so much going on that instead of tackling the problems one little piece at a time, you get despondent. Then you start worrying, you get stressed, you spend lots of energy and time worrying, and then you don't get anything done because you feel exhausted and downhearted about it all.

Take one small problem:

- **Difficult homework requiring research**
- **No research material readily available**
- **Put off doing research, find other more interesting things to do**
- **Homework deadline approaches**
- **Panic about lack of time**
- **Do nothing but waste time and avoid the problem**
- **Make excuses and reasons to avoid the issue**
- **D-Day and a detention!**

All that stress and wasted time and energy worrying and still the problem is not solved, as the homework is still to be completed, and now this workload is added to the latest lot of homework, and as ET worries, panics, and gets into such a state they can't seem to make a start. 'I can't, I can't, it's not my fault' they wail as the problem just spirals around and around, and is not going to go away until ET faces it square on. And if this homework is not completed, other work will fall behind, and then coursework starts to back up, and then the whole issue can easily become one very large ongoing problem ultimately leading to a failed exam.

The IT type

The IT type knows the work problem is within their power to solve, no-one else can do it for them, and so they get organised, work out the best solution, and take it something like this:

- **Difficult homework requiring research**
- **No research material readily available**
- **Work out where to find material (library, friend, teacher, internet etc)**
- **Work out when to get material**
- **Gather everything they need together (books, paper, pens etc)**
- **Find uninterrupted time to work (first thing in the morning, not last thing the night before the deadline)**
- **Work until homework completed, either in one go, or in blocks of good concentration time.**
- **Do their best, and give homework in on time**

The ET type

ETs — who have an external locus of control — may at some time suddenly find life seems to be spiralling totally out of control. Their misery at not feeling in charge of events could even lead to a kind of depression, which becomes worse and worse. It could also lead to what is called learned helplessness. This is where you come to believe that you can do nothing to help yourself in a certain situation. As a result you do nothing and the situation stays the same or gets worse. This backs up your view that there really is nothing at all to be done. Usually the first step up from this downward spiral is for you to recognise that the only person who can help is yourself! You must believe that there is hope and that there is something positive that can be done. By giving yourself targets to reach, or goals to achieve, however small at first, you can come to realise that your life can be anything you want to make it.

First, you need a small goal to achieve...like getting out of bed!

If you see some of ET in yourself, start trying to think positively. If you say to yourself often enough 'I can, I can' you will soon start to believe that you can. One of the ways forward is to manage your time effectively. Take a look at how much time you waste avoiding doing things which you know have to be done, but perhaps are unpleasant, or boring, or you think are too difficult. You might waste your time like this:

- **Stay up late worrying**

- **Lie in bed for longer than necessary at weekends**

- **Go out and avoid the problem**

- **Talk on the phone to friends you'll be seeing later anyway**

- **Watch television, listen to music and lie about feeling tired**
- **Spend hours in the bathroom or on your face and body**
- **Shopping for things you don't really need**
- **Start a job, not complete it, go onto the next, leave that unfinished and so on**

What else do you do? Actually writing things down or drawing them can be half way to recognising all sorts of problems, helping you to then face up to them and find solutions. Fill in this box with either words or pictures of time wasting and messing about activities:

Organise yourself

To be in control, you need to organise yourself better. Set the alarm and get up, get dressed, eat breakfast, and with a piece of paper plan your day. Set yourself little tasks, and then little treats as rewards, so your day, let's say it's a Saturday, could look like this:

- **Iron, or washing whilst watching favourite television programme**

- **Phone a friend**

- **Tidy bedroom whilst listening to music**

- **Eat lunch**

- **Ask parent if any jobs need doing/run an errand (could be combined with seeing a friend)**

- **Do a set time of homework (say 45 minutes to an hour)**

- **Take a break (take a bath, do a hobby or sport, read — whatever)**

- **Do more homework or see what else needs doing, and what time you have left to do what you want to**

- **End the day unwinding and relaxing- bake a favourite cake/ biscuits/meal, go for a cycle/swim/skate, phone a friend for a chat - one who makes you laugh (more ideas about rewarding yourself for your efforts later).**

Be flexible in your plans

The plan you draw up at breakfast may need changing as things occur throughout the day. It may be your parents plan to take you out at some point, or a friend asks you out for later. Have a look at your schedule. Juggle it. Alternatively, write out a list of things you know you really should complete. Do they need to be done today? Can some truthfully wait until tomorrow? If so, can you fit in time to do them another time? It's a question of priorities, and priorities versus stress. If you know you need to walk the dog/clean out a pet, and you'll feel bad if you don't do it, do that task first. You will feel so good about yourself. And if you know you have a deadline to do something, start by tackling that job, even if it's in bites of time. If your room is tidy, or your washing done, or you have your kit ready for school or sports, or you've actually done something you promised to do for a mate, think of how less stressed you'll feel, how less hassled you'll be by others, and you can go out and have a good time with a happy conscience. You will feel great!

Bigger stresses

No matter whether you are an IT or an ET there may be some big stresses you can do little about, and whilst they are going on, you have to look after yourself to keep as healthy and happy as possible whilst the problem continues. Big stresses could be like the work and revision leading up to exams, a house move, or a separation of some kind. It could be a death or illness of someone close to you. It could be things completely beyond your control. However these big stresses could directly affect you. You may find yourself with extra jobs or responsibilities, increased workload, listening to others who are worried.

You will need to take time out for yourself, either by finding quiet time to do things you want to do, or by going out and letting off steam, say through sport, or dancing at a music event, or by telling a friend of your worries. Recognise there is a problem, see where you fit into that problem, and start to take a positive look at ways you can help yourself. Stress can be like milk boiling in a pan, if you don't manage to turn the heat down somehow, your stress will boil over into illness or anger, depression or withdrawal.

CHAPTER 3

DOWN AND OUT

Mental health problems

As you know, no two people are exactly the same, or think the same, or tackle problems in the same way. This is probably why it is so difficult to get to the root of mental health problems and to recognise exactly what is wrong with someone. When someone's emotional well being is disturbed, every little extra problem can become too much. Their brain then suffers from overload of information, worry, stress and too much thinking as the person tries to work out what to do. But it may not be a problem one person can deal with alone, without sharing some of the burden with another. The worrier thinks themselves into a corner, and can sometimes collapse from the strain of it all and no longer function normally.

Diagnosis of a physical illness is easy compared to a mental one. It's quite straightforward to recognise a broken bone, but what about a broken heart? It's also quite easy to treat and mend a broken bone; after all it's something that can be seen on an X-ray. But it's much more difficult when you're working with things you can't see. It would be much easier if we could climb inside a person to see what was going on and try to sort out how to put it right.

Mental health problems may happen as a result of an injury or just one stressful life event, the way someone has been brought up, or an inherited problem. If the person is not able to deal with what has happened to them effectively then other problems can follow. Some people can bottle things up, or block them out completely. Some can't express their feelings easily and others either can't show any emotion at all, or become too emotional/tearful etc.

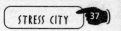

Recognising mental health problems:

- *depression*   - *breakdown*
   - *obsession*   - *phobias*
            - *panic attacks*
   - *eating disorders*
                  - *self harm*

Eating disorder! Who me?

- **Depression** (more about this later).

- **Nervous breakdowns:** a nervous breakdown is where there has been an overload in emotion. Perhaps the person has bottled things up inside for so long that their feelings finally rush out all at once (a bit like shaking a bottle of cola for a long time and then taking the lid off). This stops the person from behaving as they would usually for a time. A person may change: sleep a lot or hardly at all; behave unusually; talk too much or not at all; focus so much on an issue that they seem not to hear when you are talking to them, and then they keep going back to the same issue over and over again. A lot of people who finally crack up under pressure can't seem to concentrate on anything for very long and behave very strangely. this can be quite scary both to the person it is happening to, as well as those around.

My mum had a breakdown after a court case with my dad following their divorce. She couldn't seem to remember anything she had said or done, and would do stuff like put her handbag in the fridge because she didn't seem to know what she was doing.

(11-YEAR-OLD GIRL)

- **Phobias:** this is a big fear of a certain object, activity, animal or situation. Many people have phobias about flying in aeroplanes, spiders ('arachnophobia'), small spaces ('claustrophobia'), crowds ('agoraphobia'), or of the dark. Phobias are nothing to be ashamed about, and can all be treated and cured by medical and other experts.

Slugs and snails make me feel sick when I look at them. I couldn't touch or pick one up.

(16-YEAR-OLD BOY)

> *Steamy rooms make me feel claustrophobic and irritable. I have showers and avoid baths and saunas.*
>
> (16-YEAR-OLD BOY)

- **Obsessions:** obsessions are an unhealthy interest in a subject or a person. For example, some people become obsessed with germs and wash their hands continually. Others may become obsessed with their favourite television stars, or an ex-boy- or girlfriend, and their lives and conversations start to revolve around that person They live in a fantasy world where they truly believe things which you just know are not logical.

> *Following my friend's parents separation, she said that they'd moved to a council house because her mum had lost the keys to their mansion. She tells wild tales which just can't be true, I think it's her way of escaping from reality.*
>
> (13-YEAR-OLD GIRL)

> *My sister was crying at school, saying that my mum had had an accident, and my dad had gone off in his Lear jet to Spain with a famous model, but not to tell my mum. We'd just changed schools because she was unhappy at the last one. I was so embarrassed.*
>
> (11-YEAR-OLD BOY)

- **Self-harm / self-mutilation:** sometimes things seem so bad the person may want to hurt themselves deliberately. It's as if the focus on physical pain may take away their mental fears, or that in some way they deserve to be punished because they have overwhelming feelings of guilt or low self-worth, which may just not be justifiable. Or cutting themselves and getting medical treatment is a cry for attention as nothing else seems to be working for them. Self-harm or self-mutilation is dangerous and unhealthy, and if you or one of your friends is hurting themselves on purpose, help needs to be sought.

- **Panic attacks:** if ever you've been in a situation and have had dizziness, chest pain and sweating, felt claustrophobic (fear of being in a small space or trapped in some way) then it's more than likely you've had a panic attack. Any situation or object can spark it off if you are already stressed.

Spiders make me panic. My head goes all funny and I breathe faster as I scream. I haven't dealt with it. I couldn't imagine having one crawling on me.

(16-YEAR-OLD GIRL)

I really hate going in lifts, just the thought of them makes my palms sweat, they are too small, the cable might break, we all might get trapped or die. I know it's not logical but I'd sooner climb the stairs

(15-YEAR-OLD BOY)

- **Eating Disorders:** these can occur when someone is desperately trying to keep some kind of control or order in their lives, or may have such a low opinion of their body and themselves, that they think dieting will cure everything, or they find comfort (like a baby sucking on a dummy) in the actual pleasurable activity of eating. People may binge eat until they feel ill or sick, and may force themselves to be sick in fear and guilt of putting on weight - bulimia. Anorexia is where a person seriously controls and limits their intake of food, and can become very thin and dangerously ill. There are all sorts of ways people can use food to control themselves and others, from peculiar likes and dislikes, to positive phobias about some foods and ways of eating. It's very frightening if you see someone who doesn't eat properly getting ill and thin, and these people will need professional help to solve their mental and eating problems. If you have good mental well being, you wouldn't choose food - a source of life - as a weapon against yourself or others.

Stress and your mind

If you suddenly find you are under too much stress, whatever it may be, it can become harmful in that it stops your body and mind working properly. More and more young people are experiencing stress quite badly. This could be due to:

- **problems at home**
- **boredom**
- **school work**
- **friends**
- **exams**
- **school in general**
- **part-time jobs**
- **family**
- **illness of someone close**
- **lack of money**
- **expectations others have of you**

How do you feel when you get stressed? Like Shaz here? Anything else? Take a pencil and add your own feelings to Baz' picture.

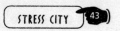

How to cope

So that's it: you feel stressed. Your pet has died, you've lost your wallet, you got a poor mark for homework, your family want to visit a sick relative when you had the chance to go to a theme park, your team lost their match, you've spilt water on your favourite photo, and just as you got in the bath to unwind, the friend whose call you have been waiting for all day rings. You are fed up, you want to cry, and you've absolutely had enough. What next?

The first thing is to think positively, and focus on the good things you do have, and know that you can cope. Think of the basic good things you might have: health, food, warmth, somewhere to sleep, home, family, friends. Think of the other good things you have in your life, or some of the things you are good at. There may be times when none of these good things seem to outweigh all the rubbish that's happening in your life. So what can you do?

Have you considered some of the following?

- cleaning/sorting out (wardrobe, photos etc)/ironing
  (yes, this works!)
- talking to someone close
- re-arranging your room
- planning something for the future (trip out —
  cinema, concert, event)
- shopping or window shopping
- catching up on missed sleep
- planning to re-decorate your room
- screaming into a pillow
- punching a cushion

- singing
- music
- walking
- happy ending video
- reading/games
- craft or hobbies
- helping someone else
- dancing
- treating yourself

- **fixing or mending something broken**
- **sport**
- **changing your image/hair etc**
- **socialising**
- **calling or contacting someone you haven't heard from in ages — could be a friend who has moved, or a cousin**
- **looking at ways to earn more money — helping at home, getting a part-time job, doing a job for a neighbour**
- **listening to someone else's problems**
- **digging the garden/growing some plants**
- **getting involved in a new group/sport/hobby**

What else can you think of which might work for you? When you feel really low, set yourself a very small goal or target and achieve it. You will then feel more able to tackle the next thing which needs doing. Don't set impossible targets. If you decided, say, to re-decorate your room, it's probably not be a job you can do in one day. It will take planning, money and time to prepare and complete the job. Every little target you reach will make you feel more positive. When things are really tough, take life hour by hour, and one step at a time. One of the best things you can do is to smile, and to laugh whether at a comedy programme or with a group of friends or family. Can you see a way of getting yourself into a fun situation?

Abuse

What if the stress isn't caused directly by more usual circumstances, but by the poor behaviour of other people? There are some things in life which may seem completely beyond your control, and will cause great fear and worry. If you are in this situation then know you don't have to go through it alone. You have the right to grow up protected. Whether the abuse is physical, mental or sexual, it should always be reported to someone you can trust. Mental abuse can be as disturbing as physical abuse. To be bullied with words, or continually criticised and put down can have a devastating effect on your morale and well being, especially if it's a constant drip-drip, nag-nag, shout yell of unfair put downs. If you are being abused, then it's not your fault. The person who is abusing you needs help. Tell someone! You will know when something is wrong, even if you just have a feeling that something is not quite right. If you wouldn't treat another person the way you are being treated, then it is probably wrong. Talk to someone else. Is the behaviour of the other person towards you normal? Do other people put up with the same things? Find out. Do not put up with events hoping the problem will go away, or thinking you deserve the treatment, or you'll be leaving the situation soon anyway. It has to stop, and now, before you or someone else becomes a victim.

Depression

Depression is a scary word. An ordinary dictionary might describe it as 'a lowering, sinking, melancholy, or a mood of hopelessness'. Real depression is more than just a mood, it can ultimately lead to a prolonged and severe illness, where a person can't function normally in society, and has feelings of suicide. Some people think depression is a nasty mental illness, or a taboo subject and not to be admitted to. There are many people who suffer from depression — more than you would expect, about one in five of the population — and it can creep up on you at any age and at any time in your life. Because it is such a strong feeling and friends and family often don't know how to react to it, people who suffer from depression usually don't like talking about it. This can lead to fear and misunderstanding and can also make it very difficult to begin to put the problems right.

In the same way that some people can't actually bring themselves to talk about death, they give different names to feelings of depression:

- **the black dog**
- **the miseries**
- **blues**
- **feeling down**
- **the pits**
- **on a downer**
- **a sad on**
- **wretched**
- **moody**
- **PMS**

Some people may say they are depressed, when really they are just having to deal with fairly small worries which make them fed up, and for others true depression can have devastating effects.

> My aunty was depressed when she had cancer. It seemed that the depression stuck with her and she didn't try to fight. She died not long after and I really believe that if she'd have fought the cancer and the depression she may have lived a bit longer.
>
> (16-YEAR-OLD GIRL)

As you hit those adolescent years, with all the new fears and feelings of growing up, you need to keep yourself fit and healthy. This means taking care of your mental and emotional health as well as your physical health. You'll probably find yourself going through lots of emotional ups and downs — where the ups are very up (you're very happy and on top of the world — whoo hoo!) and the downs are very down (periods of doom and gloom and-nobody-loves-or-understands-me!)

Mood swings are common (and there are more than just a few growing hormones interfering here) and although they're a hassle for you and the people around you, they tend not to be a major problem unless they are frequent and/or long lasting. It's during this time that facing up to the stress and problems that occur is not always easy. Remember that during this period it is vital to look after yourself emotionally. Begin to try and recognise your feelings and understand them. How are they affected by stresses, for example? It's true that very often your physical and emotional health are connected. Stress needs to be recognised and dealt with, otherwise problems, both physical and mental can occur. Usually, it's much easier to cope with and put right the physical changes that may occur due to stress. The mental problems are much harder to accept and come to terms with.

Feeling more than down

If ever you've felt depressed, then you know that it's a bit more than just feeling 'down'. You may feel like you are sinking in a swamp of despair, or a deep dark pit which you can't seem to climb out of, and even if you could see a ladder, you haven't got the energy to crawl up and out. There may also be a very strong feeling of sadness or dread that affects how you behave and feel about others and the situation you're in. If you can see no way out of the problem, then the depression can become worse and more intense. It can also last a long time.

Come on, Shaz! You've got to pull yourself out of it!

SINK!
SINK!

swamp of

Everyone is different and will react differently to each situation, but in a lot of cases depression begins with some kind of stress. This causes a 'down' in your mood which just becomes worse and worse until eventually you may feel in despair. There may appear to be no way out of the situation and no light at the end of the tunnel. If this happens and the depression changes your personality, disturbs your sleep, and your normal style of living, then the depression can become an illness. This is because long term stress can actually lead to chemical changes in the brain, which may need therapy or even drug treatment to return them to normal levels.

At this time trying to 'cheer up' the person won't help; saying something along the lines of 'It's not all that bad' will not help at all, and may depress the person even more. A depressed person will need special treatment and support. Being depressed can make you feel so bad it's untrue. You may feel worthless and that life isn't worth living. You need to accept what others may be trying to tell you, and listen to their advice and suggestions. Other people may spot your changes in behaviour before you do, and those who care for you will be trying to tell you and offer help. If ever you reach this stage, then it's important to recognise your feelings, admit and express them and don't be scared of asking for help.

Some effects of depression

If you do become really depressed and stressed then you may feel some of the following:

- **memory loss**
- **unable to string sentences together**
- **cannot concentrate**
- **self neglect**
- **change in sleep patterns**
- **change in behaviour**
- **school work is suffering**
- **no appetite**
- **no interest in anything**
- **neglect of others**
- **want to hurt yourself**
- **can't face problems**

Depression can affect the people close to the person who is suffering. We all have some influence on others around us by the way we behave and feel. A happy person who makes the smallest critical comment to someone who is depressed can result in a hurtful, barbed comment flung back at them. Depressed people can cause strains in family relationships, but it is important to remember that, to some extent, the depressed person does not always intend to hurt or trouble others.

> *There's been no one thing I can pinpoint. I've only ever been really depressed once. I watched close people around me become very upset over the loss of someone. It came to the point where I felt useless. I couldn't help them. Everything I tried to do academically and in sport didn't seem good enough. I felt as if I was letting them all down. So I didn't do anything — by doing nothing it couldn't be labelled as bad or good. I felt helpless. Then I started to feel that it might be better if I wasn't there at all. I couldn't let them down if I wasn't there ...*
>
> (16-YEAR-OLD GIRL)

Causes of depression

The number of adolescents suffering from depression is on the increase. The reasons why people become depressed will vary from person to person. You are all individuals and situations, people and stress will affect you in different ways.

There are many causes of depression. Some people believe depression is inherited from parents or grandparents. For a lot of depressed people, the cause is a hormone imbalance in their bodies, which can affect the body and brain's natural chemical balance. For some people, depression is related to illness and poor diet that doesn't give the correct amount of vitamins and iron.

As well as physical factors there are also psychological ones that can trigger off depressed feelings:

- **moving house**
- **death of someone close**
- **no money**

- **divorce of parents**
- **catastrophe or world disaster (war / famine, for example)**
- **breakdown in a relationship with parents/friends**
- **bullying**

All sorts of problems big and small affect people in different ways. Something which is a major issue for one person, could be shrugged off by another.

> Just after I split with my boyfriend of five months, I saw him kissing one of my best friends. I cried for hours after and for days. I didn't want to do anything. It was like it had just hit me that we had split up. No-one seemed to understand how I felt or what was happening. To get over it, me and my friends got together and I tore up photos of us. I still think about us a lot, but have learned to live with how it makes me feel.

(16-YEAR-OLD GIRL)

Tips on dealing with depression

Obviously there are other big life changes that can also affect you and the way you're feeling. If you ever realise that you have these negative emotions, then that's the first step towards getting better. Talk to someone you trust and get help in dealing with the way you're feeling. You will be surprised how many people will truly understand your fears and worries, but if you don't talk to someone, how will anyone know what you are going through? Support and counselling is there (see page 54) so you don't have to suffer alone or in silence. Think through who could help you, a friend, adult, school counsellor, doctor, parent. There will be someone.

If you have a friend who you know is depressed, don't just say to them, 'Snap out of it' or 'Pull yourself together'. Comments like these will just make your friend feel worse. The best thing you can do as a friend is to be there, to include your depressed friend in conversations (no matter how hard-going this might be), invite your friend round to watch videos or something. Don't ignore your friend; this will make them feel even more isolated and lonely and depressed.

Look after you

To combat stress and depression you have to believe in your own worth. Believe in you. You are amazing! It's a well known fact that having a strong self-esteem can help overcome problems. Don't be afraid to express your own feelings and deal with problems positively. Eat well and properly and take exercise. Take time out to relax, too. Do all the things that make you feel good about yourself. Be positive and know you're worth the effort.

Make a list here of all the things you are good at, or like doing, something you did to help someone else, something you got praised for. And especially, write down the things you like about yourself.

Me and My Good Bits

But what if you don't believe you are a worthwhile person? One good tip is to stand in front of a mirror every morning and say to yourself with gusto and meaning, 'I AM good! I AM worth it!'. Start small and build up to bigger things.

If you don't feel you can discuss your problems with anyone around you, there are plenty of organisations for all sorts of problems who can help, or point you in the right direction. Just a few are listed here, but your local telephone directories will list heaps of others under easily recognisable categories. There are organisations and helplines for almost everything you can think of which may be a problem for you.

- **Childline:** ☎ 0800 800 500

- **Mind Info Line:** 15-19 Broadway, London, E15 4BQ
  ☎ 0208 522 1728, *outside London:* ☎ 0345 660163

- **Saneline:** (Helpline: ☎ 0345 678000)

- **Alateen** (part of Al-Anon)**:** ☎ 020 7403 0888

- **Samaritans:** ☎ 0345 909090

- **Youth Access:** ☎ 0208 772 9900

See also useful contacts (UK) page 158

CHAPTER 4

NO PLACE LIKE HOME

Consider your situation, where you live and with whom.

The years between the ages of 11 and 16 are usually the most difficult and stressful for you in terms of personal relationships. This is true not only for you, but also for the people you live with. There may be tremendous gut wrenching arguments that flare up out of nothing in particular. Your family all suddenly start to get on your nerves, for little things that you've never noticed about them before. There will be times that seem to be far worse than others, but, of course this will vary from individual to individual.

Draw a cartoon or stick man of you in a stress. What do you say or think when someone really gets up your nose at home?

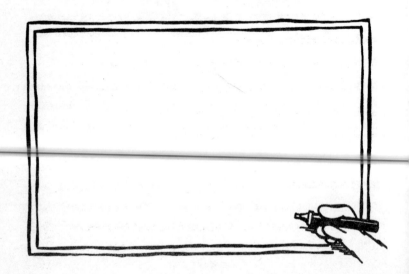

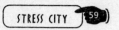

Independence days

You may find that you suddenly want more independence. Independence usually means the way you need to control and guide every aspect of your own life. You may begin to reject things you see as childish and want (no, sometimes demand!) to be treated like a grown up by others. It's a pretty confusing time, you may want to cuddle up to a parent at one moment, and run a mile should they dare kiss you goodbye in public! You may want help with a decision, and then when someone makes lots of good suggestions, you dismiss every one, and are still left undecided. Recognise any of these?

- **becoming fed up of family routine**

- **feeling misunderstood or rejected**

- **complaining about the little details of everyday life**

- **wanting to choose your own friends and clothes**

- **arguing about bedtime**

- **rather watch television or listen to music than do homework**

- **envious of older children's freedom**

- **feeling your brother/ sister gets away with murder**

- **asking why your bedroom has to be tidy**

- **asking why you have to help around the house**

- **questioning anything and everything**

- **plus... a thousand other everyday problems that suddenly seem enormous!**

I argue mostly with my dad because he always takes my brother's side. He never believes me.

(14-YEAR-OLD BOY)

I get knocked down, but I get up again

As a young adolescent you may well feel that everyone around you is trying to stop you getting your independence and wants to keep you down.

> *My dad won't let me talk during his programmes. If I do he shouts 'Will you shut up!' It's not fair because he talks during my programmes and if I complain he shouts at me.*
> (14-YEAR-OLD)

You may feel very unsure of yourself, added to which your emotions suddenly go haywire! You feel everything more intensely than you've ever done in your life and take everything very seriously. You may want to grab life with both hands. Now is the most important time and you may not give much thought to the future.

Me, me, me, me and me

It's around this time that you may also tend to ignore how others are feeling, your own views, stresses and strains seeming so huge. It's difficult for you to see the effect your dramatic mood swings, your moodiness, your snappiness and quick temper and your lack of co-operation are having on your family.

I wonder who Shaz thinks of?

ME

You may find that any tact you have suddenly flies out of the window the minute you hit adolescence. You become extremely sincere and speak your mind sometimes to such a degree that it may come over as rudeness or sarcasm. You'll know when you've got it wrong or said and done something out of order. Be honest with yourself, try to take a breath and control impulsive words and actions. Try to learn from your mistakes. You will work out by trial and error when it's safe to say something about others that they're not really going to like. Communicate your wishes assertively, not aggressively and others will understand you better and you'll find it easier to co-operate and compromise in tricky situations.

Even when you start out calmly, and have planned what you want to achieve, it's often a torture to keep things to yourself if the dialogue doesn't go as you wanted it to, and you may find words blurting out when you don't really mean them to! It's often a question of not what you say, but how you say it. And timing. Asking a parent whether you can have a lift, have a friend to stay, some extra money for a disco, and something new to wear, and now, is probably not best when mum has just come back from the supermarket laden with shopping following a night shift and badly in need of a cup of tea and two minutes with her feet up.

Another thing that suddenly becomes difficult is to say something is good, or give a 'thank you'. Adults may feel very taken for granted at this time and not at all appreciated. Comments like: 'I didn't ask to be born' or 'I wish I had a different family' aren't at all helpful. Neither are comments from adults such as, 'Don't you speak to me like that!' Find a compromise and try to meet half-way. Take a breath, and consider what you are going to say, and how the other person might be feeling before you speak.

The parent trap

What exactly do you expect from the people who care for you?

- **good physical care — food/clothes/shelter**
- **to feel valued**
- **to feel equal to those around you, e.g. brothers and sisters**
- **to be appreciated**
- **to be listened to and understood**
- **to be loved**

Anything else? Add it here —

> *I argue all the time with my parents about the lack of discipline they give my sister.*
> (14-YEAR-OLD BOY)

'And the greatest of them all is love.' This is the most important thing your carers can give you. A child who is unloved suffers both physically and emotionally. You need to feel that there's someone out there who loves you no matter how bad you feel about yourself. Very often your carers may not like you very much, but the love? Well, hopefully that's always there, to see you through your hopes and fears, joys and sadness and achievements and failures!

In times of stress you also need the support from people around, even if you become very withdrawn. It helps just to know someone is there, for the times when you want to express how you are feeling. You also want to know that someone is listening fully to you. We all need positive feedback, and a parent or someone who will make time for us makes us feel worth talking to.

No matter how out of touch you and your parents or carers seem it is important to remember that they love you or like you consistently and however much you hate to admit it, you also need them.

Arguments at this time usually blow up out of nothing at all.

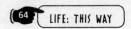
Most things argued about: these comments from 14- and 15-year-olds may sound familiar to you, too!

- **who's going to let the dog out?**
- **leaving the lights on around the house/ wasting electricity**
- **not opening your bedroom curtains**
- **not changing school clothes**
- **how long you spend on the 'phone**
- **not getting up on time in the morning**
- **leaving your school bag and shoes by the front door after school**
- **leaving stuff on the stairs**
- **getting homework done**
- **not saying where you are going, or when you'll be back**
- **time-keeping**
- **leaving the kitchen in a mess**

A world of your own

You may also find that you can live in a world of your own and detach yourself from everyone else. Any adults or family around you may continually complain that they have to say everything at least twice and then end up shouting, to get some response from you. You may not like being shouted at and you probably are in a haze as to what all the fuss is about,

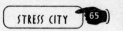

but sometimes it's the only way other people can get through! Trouble is daydreams are much more exciting than the real world!

In fact sometimes when you try to remember how an argument started , you won't be able to. It will probably end with you storming out, banging the door as loud as you can as you go. Then, alone in your room you may pass through:

resentment — justifying the way you behaved — self-pity — feeling sorry

One tip. Try not to go to bed feeling it's not sorted. Go and say, 'Goodnight' even if you can't bring yourself to say, 'Sorry.' Things look different in the morning when everyone's calmed down and they get back to normal much more quickly if you've made the effort to make the first move. Also try never to go out without saying 'Goodbye' and telling someone in your home where you will be and when you will be back, or leave a note, whatever the circumstances. It is courteous, respectful, and safety conscious. You never know when someone might need you in a hurry, or what emergency could arise.

Parents

If you're very lucky you'll be part of a family where your parents' relationship is good for most of the time with both taking an active part in the family and working together as a team. If this isn't the case then their stress may reflect in your behaviour. Your mum may become possessive, your dad, stand-offish. They may try to get you to take each other's point of view and act as go-between. Try to remember that there are two sides to every story. These are people doing their best, often making mistakes, with their own stresses and grief. What type of personalities are they? You could be an IT

personality, living with two ETs who wouldn't know a positive thought if it fell on their heads! You'll soon pick up if there are any problems. Young people tend to become very sensitive to the home atmosphere, almost like having a sixth sense!

Brothers and sisters

These relationships are another important part of family life that can very often bring you stress.

Parents will sometimes seem to favour one of you more than the other, depending on your recent behaviour! You'll be quick to realise which one of you is flavour of the month! It's also a fact that you may get on with one of your carers better than the other at different times in your life.

You'll know for a fact that when you're together with brothers or sisters it can very quickly become a war zone.

I'm forever arguing with my brother on how loud my music and the TV is. I like my music really loud, so everyone can hear it outside. My brother turns it down and I turn it back up.

(14-YEAR-OLD GIRL)

We argue about what match to have on. I support Aston Villa, my big brother supports Liverpool and my little brother supports Manchester United. we're always arguing about the nibbly little details.

(14-YEAR-OLD BOY)

Younger brothers and sisters can be a real pain, following you everywhere, wanting to do what you do. Annoying, interrupting, and teasing. You may dread the words, 'Take your brother / sister with you!' when uttered by your parents just as you are about to go out.

Me and my brother argue the most about who has the TV remote!

(14-YEAR-OLD BOY)

But there are advantages. Having brothers and sisters makes you realise that you can't always have your own way and that there are other people to be considered. You will have to share things with others throughout your life, compete at times and deal with unfairness. A lot of learning can be done at home learning to communicate with others. Many brothers and sisters will fight like cat and dog, but stick up for each other against other people no matter who they are. They can also become great supporters for you at school and at home. They can also help you develop patience and understanding.

Another way they can stress you out is if they are older than you, and decide to leave home. This can hit the ones left behind like a sledgehammer. Even if you can't wait for them to go at first. When they actually have, there may seem to be a big hole left in your life and you're loathe to admit that, yes, you do miss them.

Only you?

As an only child, you're the centre of your parents' affection. Usually being the only one means you get more attention, and even that more money can be spent on you. You also get more privacy and a even a room of your own! Usually school and surroundings provide you with friends that offer enough companionship.

But with the advantages come disadvantages. Many people say that the main disadvantage to being an only child is that you miss out on the social side of having other young people around you and you don't learn how to share. Whether or not this is true depends a lot on personal circumstances and you and your parents' attitudes.

Chores

Some of the day to day running of a home, and living and interacting with those around you can cause a lot of grief and stress, and create war-zone home situations! God forbid you should clean the car! You can't even keep your own room tidy. People who enter do so at their peril and risk broken limbs and sometimes asphyxiation. Time is far too precious to waste doing sissy housework, cooking or helping out!

> The thing I argue with my mum about is making a cup of tea. She never makes one, not even for herself. She always makes me do the drinks, even if I'm in the bath she makes me get out to make her a drink.

(14-YEAR-OLD GIRL)

Besides which, if you do help, you'll expect a vast amount of praise for doing it and you'll realise that you may actually be doing more than a brother or sister (not allowed). In time you wake up. Although it's not enjoyable most of us realise it actually causes less stress if you play it fair and do your bit! Running a home, keeping things clean, tidy and as easy as possible for everyone to move around and find stuff takes a lot of work. If everyone in the house does a share, it's easy to keep things smooth and stress free. But if everything gets dumped on, or done by only one or some of the household members, then there's an explosion of resentment waiting to happen. What do you get moaned at about most at home? Which causes you more stress: doing a task efficiently when asked, or not doing it, or doing it badly? Make two lists. One of moans, one of things you don't mind doing. Can you do the worst first? Or volunteer to do some of the things you are good at, or like?

I argue with my mum about what time to be in and what jobs I have to do around the house.

(13-YEAR-OLD GIRL)

Your stuff

As you get further into the teenage years you become very attached to your own things, sometimes passionately so. Not just things bought for you by parents or others, but especially things you've bought with your own money. They become treasures to be collected and protected. Clothes, music, pens, little things that have sentimental value. You may want to guard these items fiercely against all intruders. They will usually be kept in the inner sanctum of your bedroom, which is very much your space and territory.

Most arguments? Tidying my room. My mum doesn't understand that I LIKE my mess and if it goes I wouldn't be the same person.
(14-YEAR-OLD BOY)

I argue with my sister if she touches my CDs or wears my clothes. She also turns the TV channel over when I'm watching a programme.
(13-YEAR-OLD GIRL)

Wrinklies — the aliens

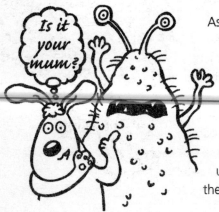
Is it your mum?

As you move from childhood to adulthood you gain more independence, and learn more about responsibility and the ways of adult life. You may begin to put all adults under the microscope. You start to make up your own mind about them and sometimes you won't be very impressed with what you find. You'll call their ideas and opinions into question until they've justified them well enough for you. You may also feel that you're losing some respect for some adults. Generally it's true that you're more likely to respect adults who admit they're wrong or unfair on occasion. It's also true that you may not be able to forgive adults who refuse to admit they could be wrong or unfair.

When you are small, you believe most things that the big grown ups tell you, and accept their judgement without question. As you get older and wiser, you will realise that all adults are not perfect, they may be mad, bad, angry, opinionated, boring or just plain wrong. How you answer them, or how you deal with them will depend on each individual situation, and how to get away with the least stress or grief for all involved.

Home time?

A lot of arguments stem from what time to be home at night. Your friends seem to be able to stay out later than you and you're frightened to death of having to go home and miss something! This could make you feel that adults don't trust you, giving you set times to be in, warnings and direct no-go areas. Your friends are out and about and usually in a big group, so you can't see any harm in it. It may come across as unfair if your rules are different from everyone else's.

Come on, home time! You won't miss anything here!

Baz!

DRAG!

In truth they probably aren't all that different, it just seems that way. Other parents may care less about their children than yours do, or be weaker and more easily manipulated because of their own stresses and problems. The fact of the matter is that you'll probably feel resentful when adults give you a lecture on why you can't stay out late. Being treated like a child is another feeling you may have. Your parents, though don't want you hurt and they want to know where you are and exactly what time you'll be home. So they know when to start worrying. Try to see it from their point of view. Rules aren't there to stop you having fun. It's not down to mistrust, either (although trust takes time to build up, so it's wise not to abuse it when it's given to you!) It's because deep down they care, and want you home safely in one piece. It's as simple as that!

CHAPTER 5

FRIENDS WHO'LL BE THERE FOR YOU

It's alright for a while - but I need my family and friends

BAZ-
NO
MATES

Mates

Feeling that you belong to a group is very important. Humans were not meant to live alone, but with others in teams, with friends and believe it or not, family groups! To live healthily, we need people. A solitary existence may be alright for a while, but most people need the support, stimulation and company of other mates. If you ever get rejected by a friend, or a group, make sure you have another to fall back on and help you through any difficult situations. If you have fallen out with your closest mates or those around you, you will need either to make the peace, or find other supporters until the dust has settled. A broken friendship, or relationship can lead to greater worry, stress and emotional pain than anything else in life.

Friends are important to us through life, and coping with friendships and peer pressure is a big part of life's learning curve. You learn skills that you need for adulthood, get to know yourself a little better and realise that there are some things that you consider important despite what others may think.

Friends stress me out when they cheek me and then say they're still my friend. I don't think so!
(13-YEAR-OLD BOY)

Friendly stress

You probably have a close group of friends and you may also belong to some kind of club where you all go to enjoy yourselves or just relax. Most people also have one or two really close friends to natter to about absolutely anything at all for hours on end.

Your parents' attitudes to your friends can also affect relationships. You don't take kindly to being told that a certain person is no good for you and you may find that you're driven to stick with them even more closely than you otherwise would.

But a lot of stress can be caused by friendships or fallings out. For girls especially, friendships play an important part of their lives because of the deep feelings that are present. That isn't to say that friendship isn't so important for boys, but they may find it harder to express their feelings. Boys also tend to sort out any disagreements in a physical way and then get on with the friendship! Girls tend to handle things more psychologically, which can be much more damaging in the long run for all the individuals concerned.

Things which stress out friends can include the following, from 13 and 14-year-olds:

- **when they copy me**
- **when they try to make out they're better than me**
- **being two-faced**
- **when they tell others your secrets**
- **when they lie about you**
- **when they tell other people who you fancy**
- **when they put me down and make me feel unhappy**
- **their changing mood swings**
- **when they boss me about**
- **when they make me feel bad**
- **when clothes look better on them**
- **when they have loads more money**
- **when they're prettier than me**
- **when they're cleverer than you and don't think they are**
- **when they take twice as long as me to get ready and I have to sit and wait**
- **when you're all with a group of bigger kids that they know and you don't and they cheek you**
- **when we arrange to meet after lessons — they hardly ever wait!**

You may worry about a lot of the things that are talked about in the problem pages of magazines:

Dear Agatha Agony Aunt
I've just moved to a new area, and haven't met any new friends yet. What can I do? We've been here a week now and being alone and missing my old friends is really stressing me out.
Yours Gregory Gregarious

See, its not so bad!

Dear Gregory
First check out your local paper, community notice boards, library and so on to see what's on in your area. There is probably something you'd like to join or try ranging from a drama group, to sea cadets, to discos, to skating. You'll probably find friends there who live near you. When you start your new school, there's bound to be people in your class who will become good mates, and others in activities run by the school. You could take a part time job, even delivering the free papers locally would help you to get to know the area, and you may bump into others of your age. To break the ice, it's worth being brave, smiling, and saying hello to people. That's often all it takes to start up a conversation. Agatha's words of the day are: most strangers are just friends we haven't yet met. Go get 'em, Ags

Other friendship stresses include:

- **rejection**
- **family not liking friends**
- **faults in friends**
- **boyfriend/girlfriend problems**
- **being dumped**
- **how to attract the opposite sex/make them fancy you**
- **jealous boy/girlfriend**
- **critical girl/boyfriend**
- **how to get rid of your girl/boyfriend**
- **sex and pregnancy**
- **group or gang of friends pressures**
- **money**

Peer pressure

You've probably realised by now that your friends have a lot if influence over you during this stage of your life. Look at the clothes you wear, the labels in them, the things you like to eat, the music you listen to. All of these things are open to the influence of others even if you're not aware of it. The kind of pressure you get as a teenager will be different to the peer pressure you get as an adult.

In adulthood, it's very often not as important to be 'one of the gang'. By this time you've found out who you are, and care less what others think. But when you are younger, it's vital!

Most of us want to be one of the gang and not do anything to stand out. We tend to obey the unwritten rules of the group without thinking about it. You may feel pressurised into doing things

you don't want to, like smoking, shop-lifting, not taking studies seriously, sexual activity, drugs, vandalism.

But you have a choice about who you hang around with, and whether you do as they say. You don't have to fall into just any group - you can choose friends who like what you like and think the same way. You can find mates with interests in common, and who share similar views on things and people.

> *Friends stress me out when I ask them to do something or remember something and they either forget or don't do it. Some of my friends are a lot prettier than me and always moan about how ugly they are or fat. The truth is they look perfect.*
>
> (14-YEAR-OLD GIRL)

Sometimes, though, you need to stand up for yourself and trust your own judgement if the group is doing things that you are not happy with.

Too much pressure

Sometimes peer pressure can get too much for some people. Being part of a group can often mean that your needs as an individual are being ignored. Life can then become difficult as you feel unable to function as a person.

I get stressed when my friends can't accept that I want to do other things. Not always what they want me to do!

(14-YEAR-OLD BOY)

And you know the effects of stress upon stress!

As you get older and into your teenage years you may find it more and more difficult to talk about your feelings to any adult, either at home or at school. It's easier to talk to your best friends who have the same hopes and stresses. Although this is the case and friends can be a great source of comfort to you, it's also important to remember that they can also be a great source of your stress! Keeping them happy, not falling out with them, and yet trying to retain your own respect and identity can be pretty wearing.

 *My best friend is prettier than me and always has more money, nice clothes and a boyfriend. Sometimes she can be a bit over the top and sometimes she can't keep a secret. I often need a break from her. Sometimes when she's joking she doesn't know that she's being quite nasty.*

(13-YEAR-OLD GIRL)

Friends versus family

The friends you chose for yourself are not always the ones your family would chose for you. Particularly once you get into the boyfriend/girlfriend thing! You may feel quite touchy about adults' attitudes to your mates. Problems may occur when you bring friends home. What if your family says something to embarrass you, or make it clear they don't like someone? Or perhaps it's your friend whom you feel lets you down in some way when you want your family so much to like them On the other hand, you may take someone home who is quite different from previous friends they have known in order to shock them and take notice of you. Part of growing up is being rebellious, and pushing others to their limits of tolerance.

The truth is if you know your family isn't too keen on one of your mates then this can make you react in one of two ways:

- You argue with your family. What right have they got anyway to 'butt in', you may ask yourself?

- You become fiercely loyal to your friend. After all, your family doesn't know him or her like you do.

Whilst you may think you are right about a friends character, it's often worth bearing in mind what other people say, even if you just file the information away. Time will tell whether they were right or wrong, and if your friend can be trusted.

We don't approve of your latest friend, Baz!

You can make up your own mind about them. No-one can do that for you. You may find out that your family was right after all. Or they may realise it's they that have made the mistake and welcome your friend after a while. If you realise at a later date you were wrong about someone, (maybe they were an ET, not an IT like you after all) learn from the experience and remember what to watch for in the way people behave in the future. It's desperately stress-ful and upsetting if you find out someone you believed in has lied or done something behind your back, but recognise the mistake and move on.

Of course the same goes for friends of your own friends or your own family's friends. You may make a judgement about them that you find hard to keep to yourself. Be tactful and try to remember how you felt if anyone ever criticised your choice of mates.

Home truths

You may also begin to notice at this time a difference between your friend's home and yours. You may start to compare their furnishings, the food they eat, the presents they give with yours. It may become painfully obvious that, yes, they are better off than you. But concentrate on your half full glass of milk, not the half empty one, and count up the good things you do have. True friends won't rub your nose in it. Saying that, it's still difficult to watch your friend being given the same present that it's taken you two years to save up for. Or watch them swan off abroad every year for their hols, while you're off camping again in sunny England! This is a fact of life and will always happen — even when you get into adulthood!

NEWCASTLE-UNDER-LYME
COLLEGE LEARNING
RESOURCES

CHAPTER 6

THANKS, BUT NO THANKS

In any situation that you meet in life you usually have several choices about how you can behave. The way that you react in everyday life to normal things that are going on can also add to your stress levels. The most important key to a more stress free existence is control. The more you feel in control of situations, or able to control your part in them, the less stressed you will be

Confidence and assertiveness

Have you ever been asked to do something which is unfair or unreasonable, and while you said 'yes' at the time, you have then agonised for hours as to why? It may be that someone asked to borrow something you didn't really want to lend, or to do something which would add too much pressure to your busy time. You wish you'd said 'No' and then briefly explained why whilst sticking to your reasons, or 'Thanks, but no thanks'.

People types

People tend to fall into three main types. Which 'type' are you, do you think?

1. Passive people

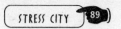

If you are passive, you hope that you get what you want, but leave it to chance. You don't always feel able to say what you want. Perhaps you are shy. You may feel quite strongly about things inside, but don't want to upset anyone. This type of person may feel so unimportant, they believe that their needs don't count. This is all well and good, but you may later regret that you let opportunities pass, or get annoyed with yourself for doing nothing. You could end up feeling bitter and resentful which may give you tendencies to 'blow up' at any moment.

Tick the following descriptions if they apply to you most of the time:

Passive people do:

- **Rely on others to guess what it is they want**
- **Sit on their feelings and try not to let them out**
- **Sigh / sulk / daydream and wish a lot**
- **Sometimes feel trampled on**

Passive people don't:

- **Ask for what they want outright**
- **Express their feelings to those who matter**
- **Feel good about themselves a lot of the time**
- **Keep busy**

How many of the above dos and don'ts apply to you? More than half and you need to take some positive action!

Passive people have breaking points too, and sometimes when they are pushed too far can explode in a spectacular way — which is not very good for anyone's stress levels.

2. Aggressive people

You are an aggressive type of person if you tend to express your feelings with force, so much so that the person you're talking to feels threatened or put down. You may be sarcastic, verbally violent or sly. The trouble is even if you win in situations you tend to leave others with a bitter feeling and a strong desire for revenge! So, although it seems like you've won in the short term, it can affect your future relationship with the other person involved.

Aggressive people do:

- **Try any way to get what they want**

- **Don't mind making others feel bad**

- **Threaten / bully / use sarcasm /**

  fight and use people

Aggressive people don't:

• **Respect others**

• **Look for a middle ground or compromise**

3. Assertive people

Assertive behaviour lets other people know how you feel without you being too passive or too aggressive. It also means that you take responsibility for yourself rather than going along with the crowd for an easy life or not to appear different.

Being assertive is a lot different to being aggressive. You're assertive if you're able to tell someone what you want or would like without threatening them or punishing them in some way. You have respect for others and don't trample over their needs, rights or feelings. You can express positive feelings and express anything negative in a good light. You're also able to stand up for yourself and your rights without taking away anyone else's.

Assertive people do:

- **Ask for what they want**

- **Look for a middle ground or compromise**

- **Believe in themselves**

- **Ask confidently and diplomatically**

- **Behave in an open and direct way**

Can we come to some agreement?

I want this – how can it be done?

I believe it can be done!

Assertive people don't:

- **Expect others to guess what you want**

- **Get worried or anxious unnecessarily**

- **Make others feel bad.**

You're not a whimp!

You know where you stand with me!

I'm cool!

Being assertive

Being assertive should be the ideal personality type for everyone. And it is possible for passive or aggressive types to change. Being assertive means you are able to show positive feelings, such as:

- **starting conversations;**
- **receive compliments without being embarrassed;**
- **telling someone you appreciate them; and**
- **give compliments.**

You can also show negative feelings:

- **that you are hurt by what someone has said or done;**
- **that you are annoyed.**

You can stand up for yourself by:

- **refusing to be put down;**
- **giving your opinion;**
- **making valid complaints; or**
- **refusing when asked to do something you don't want to do.**

What to do

There are certain tricks that you can learn to help you to be more assertive and cut your stress levels.

Decide what it is you want and make sure it's a reasonable request. Ask calmly and be positive, pointing out the benefits of your suggestion. Avoid anger and criticism, it won't get you anywhere. Repeat your request until you feel you've been heard. Of course you won't always get what you want. You may have to compromise and talk things through until you've found a middle ground.

I want to go for a walk!
The walk will do me good!
The walk will do you good!
We will get some fresh air if we go for a walk!
Let's go for a walk, now!

Whenever we meet someone else on a day to day basis we communicate with them in two main ways: verbal (spoken) and non-verbal (unspoken).

Verbal communication

Be direct and know what you want to achieve at the start of your conversation. This doesn't mean that you have to be aggressive, just know what your goal is and what you want as the end result.

- Use 'I' and take responsibility. This also shows honesty.

- Don't say 'sorry' or give apologies or explanations when they're not needed.

Remember that by saying what you want or what you believe may not be the right thing at the time for everyone else. They may have different wants and beliefs and you'll have to compromise.

Limit your use of the words 'should', 'must' and 'always'. These are more like orders than requests and can sound critical.

Non-verbal communication

Eye contact is one of the most powerful forms of communication. Direct eye contact can show confidence, lowering of the eyes may show defence while a fixed and staring gaze shows aggression.

Your facial expression must match what is being said and your expression must be genuine. There's no point at all in saying 'sorry' with a big cheesy grin on your face. It won't work!

Your posture can also say a lot about you. Leaning forward into a person can show power and status (that you're 'better' in some way than others) and may be regarded as aggressive. An upright pose shows you're relaxed. Slouching gives others the impression that you lack confidence.

Keep your gestures (usually hand movements) natural and relaxed. Twiddling or fiddling shows you're worried or nervous about something. Pointing your fingers or making fists can show you're angry or can signal aggression.

Your voice can make a difference to how people see you. Make sure it's about the right volume pitch, not too loud (aggressive) and not too soft (passive). Say 'umm', 'err' and 'emms' as little as possible, too.

Check yourself out

For the rest of the day, or for tomorrow, take a look at and listen to yourself. At the end of the day, make a note, and compare your behaviour to the types of communication above. What have you found? Is there anything you'd like to change, or improve on?

Putting it into Practice

Obviously being assertive will depend on the situation that you find yourself in. There are 'fors' and 'againsts' for dealing with a stressful situation straight away:

For:

• **feelings are dealt with there and then, no build up of frustration**

• **no risk that the issue will never be put right, if dealt with at the time.**

Againsts:

• **feelings may run high, cooling off may be necessary.**

• **it may be very public.**

• **the person may be too busy to listen to you.**

I need feeding NOW! Or I'll get really stressed!

The Situation

Examples of behaviour

- Borrowing something without asking

- Using a threat to make you do what they want
- Refusing to take 'no' for an answer

How to deal with it assertively

- Recover the object. Say 'no' and that you don't want it to happen again
- Call their bluff. Tell an adult

- Give reasons why you can't. If that doesn't work keep repeating it's not possible.

Assertiveness rules, ok?

It's important to remember that you don't have to be assertive all of the time. Learn how to judge how important the issue is for you. Think of a problem you have had and apply this 10 point scale:

8+ **Very important**—*you need to say something*

5–7 **Important**—*but you could let it pass*

1–4 **Of little importance**—*is it worth saying anything?*

Of course, some days getting a cold cup of coffee in a cafe may rate as '9', at other times you may see it as a '2'! It depends on your mood and the time and place, what kind of day you are having and how stressed you feel.

Assertive behaviour means that your relationships with others will be more open and straight forward. The way you deal with people is better and they'll know where they stand with you. You can protect your own interests when others are being aggressive, too. Being assertive is an important part of taking responsibility for yourself. It can help to develop the image you have of yourself and most importantly can help to reduce your stress levels. So, to recap:

Make clear and direct contact...

- Pick your time and place to act assertively. If you're busy, angry or jealous, wait!

- Know what you want before being assertive. State it clearly.

- Make clear and direct eye contact and try not to show you're nervous.

- Talk things through and compromise with the other person.

- Be consistent in what you're saying. Respect the views of others and be genuine.

- Check and re-check your body language, breathing and posture, for example, don't fold your arms, point your finger, raise your voice.

School days

School is stressful. There are bound to be aggressive types and passive types in every class. But luckily there are also people who are simply assertive.

It can often be difficult to be assertive at school, not with people your age, but with adults in that environment. Assertiveness can be mistaken for being cheeky or aggressive, so be aware of this and tread very carefully. Think before you open your mouth.

Make the most of the positive, kick out the negative

Some useful tips to reduce the stress in your life even further would be useful, wouldn't they? Try the following and see how much better you feel about yourself and others!

Don't label yourself, or believe labels other people give you. Assertive people often get labelled 'pushy' or 'bossy', which may stop you from being assertive in the future. People who give you these labels are probably afraid of your openness and directness.

Try to push out all negative thoughts and replace them with positive ones. Focus on positive things that have happened to you in the past. Forget the negative ones.

Build up techniques to get you through situations where you know you've got to be assertive. Plan it ahead and plan out what you need to say and do, things won't always go exactly to plan, but by keeping calm, it'll give you time to think.

If you make a mistake, it's not the end of the world. Work out why it happened and see what you've learned from it. And remember, tomorrow gives you a chance to start afresh.

Other labels may also stop you being assertive. If you're known as a 'hard worker' and 'reliable', then saying 'no' to a task may go against these labels. You know your limits, so say 'no' if you think you won't be able to cope. It'll save your stress level from going through the roof. Don't accept the labels - good or bad

Try not to imagine bad things happening if you were to assert yourself. ('If I say that, then this will happen, then this' and so on.) If you take this view then nothing will change.

Above all, remember that you have the right to be you. Respect yourself and others and you'll be a lot happier with life. Let's revisit that first scene:

CHAPTER 7

UPS AND DOWNS

Way to go... NOT!

Some people get so stressed out that they'll try anything to ease their pain, or to avoid reality. They don't see that there are other ways to deal with issues or worries and resort to taking stimulants or depressants. Maybe someone they know suggests it at first, perhaps they know someone who uses drink or drugs and seems to escape their problems and worries.

Drink

Alcohol is a legal drug and people have been making and drinking it for thousands of years. The making and selling of alcohol is controlled by governments world-wide. It's big business and keeps millions of people in a job. Use it like an idiot though, and you're in trouble. Not only do you risk hangovers, but also accidents, health and personal problems, addiction and even early death. Alcohol will have a greater effect on you as a young person because your body is more sensitive and less able to cope.

The first time I got really drunk was when I was on holiday with my friends. We could drink all we wanted because it was free! I didn't have a hangover the next day, but I found out I did some embarrassing things!

(17-YEAR-OLD)

What it is

There are four main types of alcoholic drinks: beers, wines, spirits and liqueurs. These are all made from agricultural products (hops, grapes, barley, fruits and so on) and the amount of alcohol found in each type of drink is different. Beer contains about 5% while spirits can be up to 50%. It's not safe to drink alcohol in its pure form of ethanol or ethyl alcohol; the body can only cope when the alcohol is diluted.

The more alcohol there is in a drink, the more effect it has on your body and the more out of control you will soon be. This is because alcohol changes the way your body works and can make people behave and feel completely different.

What it does

Is alcohol a harmless drug, though? Alcohol alters the normal state of your mind and your body. The effects on your mind last a matter of hours, the effects on your body could be permanent and there forever. Too much alcohol has a poisonous action in the short and long term and can lead to serious illness and even death. Common alcohol related illnesses damage the liver, kidneys and the heart.

A glass of wine, a small beer and a measure of spirits all contain about one unit of alcohol. After about two units, you're over the legal limit to drive because at this point your body and brains' ability to think and act quickly and clearly are already impaired.

Some of the other effects of alcohol are:

- **Brain:** you can forget things and find you can't think or reason clearly. The alcohol is also a depressant, which means it has the opposite effect to what you would think. This is because at first the alcohol holds down the calming bits in your brain, so you become more excited and hyper. But after a short while you'll feel the depressant effects and may become weepy or even aggressive.

- **Heart:** alcohol makes your heart beat faster, putting more pressure on it and causes the blood to travel more quickly around your body.

- **Stomach:** alcohol can upset your stomach, in excess this can lead to damage and stomach ulcers.

- **Liver:** the liver has to switch to overtime to rid the body of the toxins contained in alcohol. If overworked for a long time, it just may stop working altogether.

Alcohol can make you feel out of control, happy or sad, depending on your mood. The more you drink the clumsier you'll become. Alcohol can also affect how and what you understand. It will also affect your speech - you know how people slur their words when they've had a lot to drink. People who've had a drink seem stupid and get confused.

If you do drink a lot then you're likely wake up with a 'hangover' the next morning. This headache and sick feeling is your body's way of telling you that you overdid it. Too much alcohol and your brain loses water (dehydrates). Not a nice feeling. Way too much alcohol and you can actually poison yourself and land up in hospital risking death or serious physical and mental damage.

> *The first time I got drunk was when I was 14. I had a couple of glasses of cider. I can't remember most of the night and my hangover lasted the entire weekend. I couldn't eat anything without feeling like I was going to be sick. I've never got that drunk since. I do still enjoy an occasional drink, but I stay away from cider.*
>
> (17-YEAR-OLD)

Most people do get drunk at one time or another, some see it as part of growing up - a rite of passage. But it's also an abuse of your body, which you need to keep sane, safe and healthy.

Poisoning yourself is not really so clever.

That wasn't a good idea!

So with all these bad points about what alcohol does to you, why do people drink at all? There are many reasons:

- **adverts make it attractive**
- **feeling less shy and awkward**
- **makes people feel more grown up**
- **in religious ceremonies**
- **helps people feel they belong to a group**
- **makes them feel light-headed and happy**
- **relaxes or calms them down**

- **hospitality**
- **friends do**
- **social reasons**
- **celebration**
- **makes them laugh**
- **in cooking**

Saying this, it must be remembered that there are some people who just don't like the taste of alcohol or the effect it has on them. Some people are actually allergic to the yeasts and chemicals in alcoholic drinks. Just one glass can make them really sick and ill, and even behave totally out of character. Many people manage quite well all through their lives without the need for any drink containing alcohol.

Drink as a habit

Problems can crop up if you get into the habit of drinking alcohol. If you drink regularly then you get a tolerance of it and need more and more to get the same feelings. Some people get to the stage where they feel they can't do without it and depend on it too much. At the first sign of stress, or if anything goes wrong, they turn to alcohol. This addiction can lead to:

- **bad moods;**
- **fights;**
- **accidents;**
- **mood or personality changes;**
- **physical damage to the body;**
- **alcoholism;**
- **money problems - it's expensive**

Who put this lamp post here?

Drink as a problem

Drinking alone can be a problem, so too can drinking with a group. Behaviour can get rowdy or even aggressive as you egg each other on. People die as a result of alcoholic brawls, or choking on their own vomit. This can also be a danger at parties. Here people drink too much and too quickly, often to keep up with everyone else, or because they are new to the experience. Big mistake!

> *I know somebody who had to go into hospital to have their stomach pumped from alcohol poisoning at their birthday party. Although I never saw them in hospital they did 'phone me up to tell me how horrible it was to have this done. The whole experience sounded so terrible. I know my friend hardly drinks at all, now. It put me off, too!*
>
> (17-YEAR-OLD)

Drinking and driving

Drinking and driving should never be attempted. The problem is, once you've had a drink, you actually feel as though you're in control. You're not. This can be a real problem and could end in a serious accident. If you do drink and drive you risk losing your driving licence at best, and harming or killing someone and going to prison at worst. And never accept a lift from someone who has been drinking however persuasive they are.

Adverts for alcohol don't do us any favours. They make drinks seem tempting and smart. They say, 'It's cool to drink.' Rubbish.

Long-term damage report

Over a long period of time alcohol can seriously mess up your life:

- **depression**
- **throat and stomach cancer**
- **high blood pressure**
- **pancreas damage**
- **vitamin deficiency**
- **violence and abuse**
- **memory loss**
- **liver disease**
- **stomach ulcers**
- **nerve damage**
- **reduced fertility**

Needing more and more alcohol leads to the person becoming an 'alcoholic': there's a physical and mental dependence on it. The fact is that anyone can become an alcoholic, there's no age limit. While it seems to affect more men than women, that gap is closing. Don't be fooled. Alcohol is a powerful drug. Drinking it can take over your life. If you look up Alcoholism in a family medical book, you will find some frightening facts, figures and consequences of drinking too much alcohol. The book will also tell you other signs to recognise in others who you think may have a drink problem.

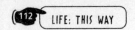
The costs of drinking too much are expensive, whether in terms of your health, your relationships, your self-esteem, and even the huge amounts of money it takes to fund a drink habit. Not really worth it to get over a bit of stress, is it?

Coping

People who are worried and upset often drink, but the problem doesn't go away. The fact is that alcohol can make things worse. It'll still be there after the hangover.

Friends can help. Talk it over with them, instead of having a drink. If you realise you're in too deep to help yourself, then join an organisation or a support group. Your doctor can help put you in touch, or look out for leaflets at medical centres.

Alcohol and the law

How does the law on the use of alcohol affect you?

- **The sale of alcohol is prohibited to under 18s.**

- **It is illegal to buy alcohol for under 18s.**

- **People under 14 are not allowed in pubs.**

- **Over 16s can have beer or cider with a meal in a restaurant.**

> *My friend stayed at [my house] after she'd had too much to drink at a party. She was drinking her cup of tea and was sick in the cup. Then she went to our loo and was sick all up the wall, turned around and smashed a glass on the floor accidentally. When we got to bed, she woke me up trampling all over me, shouting that she was locked in the room. Then she went to the loo, turned the wrong way and fell down our stairs. Luckily she was ok. The next morning she thought it had all been a dream. Yeah, right! It was a long time before she stayed at our's again.*

(17-YEAR-OLD)

Cigarettes

Cigarettes are not cool. You know all about cigarettes, you've seen the clever adverts, you know the price, you've smelt the T shirt the morning after being at a smoky place. You know they are poisonous, you know they are addictive. Once hooked — and all it takes is the occasional cigarette — you are literally sucked in. It is said that giving up a cigarette addiction is more difficult than coming off hard drugs. Cigarettes can ruin your finances, they can kill you. One cigarette may seem like a distraction, but the calm feeling you may think it brings is temporary and there are lots of little built in poisons ready to make you want another one, until the only way you think you can keep from being stressed out is to have another.

No thanks! They damage your health!

Let's leave it to some 16 and 17-year-olds to tell you what they thought:

> The first and only time I tried smoking was at a friend's house. She was trying to teach me to inhale the smoke. I have never felt so ill in my whole life. My friend still has the photo of me lying on the settee, completely white, looking like I might throw up at any second. I felt really sick for the rest of that day.

> The first cigarette I ever tried was one I stole from my brother. He never found out so I took a few more. I smoked because my friends did, and started when I was about 14. I stopped at the beginning of this year and now I'm glad I did. It smells and it's disgusting.

> I hate smoking because my dad is addicted to nicotine. I hate the way it makes the house smell and how it is making my dad, he carries his fags around like his life depends on them. I can see how totally dependent he is on cigarettes to 'calm his nerves'. I have never tried smoking as a result, because I've only seen the unglamorous side of it.

The first time I tried a fag it was absolutely disgusting. But the nicotine 'rush' that makes you feel light headed was quite nice and made me interested in them, so I began smoking. 6 months later, I realised how pathetic it was, how expensive and horrible. I quit and haven't had a drag since then.

I tried a cigarette because most of my friends smoke. I didn't find it disgusting or horrible, just nothing special. I couldn't see the point in wasting my money on something I didn't enjoy. There was no peer pressure to smoke, if you didn't want to, no-one tried to pressure you into it. they just accept it.

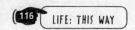

Drugs are not a solution

Many people turn to alcohol, cigarettes and drugs when they're under any stress, but these are not the answer to any stress-related problem. In fact, it can actually cause more problems for you and make the existing ones worse. All you'll get is a brief break from the problems, but once the drugs or alcohol have worn off, the problems won't have gone away. They'll still be there — waiting for you to deal with them. You know drugs and drink are expensive, sometimes illegal, often dangerous, and the effects can lead to other problems both behavioural and physical.

So what's to be done? This very much depends on the individual person and the situation they are in. But in your heart, you'll know when you've got a problem that's too big for you to handle. If you find yourself stuck in a drink or drugs trap, you know you can't cope with it alone, first you have to face up to the facts and then you've got no choice but to ask for help somewhere else. Your own doctor, or a counsellor are the best bets, or speaking to someone close and asking them to help you find a way out.

But help is

Sometimes the doctor will prescribe drugs to help you through. It's important to remember, though that these drugs will only control the way you're feeling and will help you to feel a little better, or not so worried. What they can't and won't do is to cure the problem. They may help you to feel well enough to deal with it, though.

Counselling and talking to a person outside your situation may also help you to get to the root of the problem. Talking things through very often brings up areas you hadn't thought of and ways to solve

issues that just hadn't occurred to you whilst stuck in a spiral of misery. Even so, it can take a long time for the person to realise exactly what their problem is and how to deal with it. If you have a friend with a drink or drugs problem, you may find that you can't help them or talk them out of it. They have to realise the problem for themselves. Stay out of their mess, don't let them talk you into helping them get the drugs they think they need, or taking drink or drugs with them. Say no, however they try to influence you. Only that way can you be a real friend who can stick by them if they do try to help themselves.

CHAPTER 8

FALSE CRUTCHES

The Drugs Don't Work

> I was really shocked when a girl in our village admitted that she was on drugs. Not just the soft stuff. She's on cocaine. She's the same age as me and every time I see her she looks worse. She's so thin, and has all these sores on her face. She comes from a good home, too. She used to be dead pretty, now it's obvious pretty soon she'll just be dead.

(17-YEAR-OLD BOY)

Drugs can drag you down

There are many different types of drugs that you'll come across in life. A drug is anything that you put into your body that changes or affects how your body works. Some drugs are an accepted part of life, such as tea, coffee and chocolate. Others are more powerful, but are also accepted, such as alcohol and nicotine. There are some drugs or substances that aren't designed for people to take, like glue or lighter fluid.

A lot of drugs are helpful and can be bought, such as painkillers. More powerful drugs are limited and are given out by doctors on prescription to help ill people get well. They can stop you getting diseases. You're breaking the law if you take these more powerful drugs without a prescription from your doctor.

Heroine, cocaine, amphetamines and cannabis are all illegal drugs, mainly because if they are misused they are killers.

How drugs affect your body

The effects of drugs vary, depending on the individual, the amount of the drug and how used the person is to taking it. Sometimes the effects last for minutes, sometimes for hours or even days.

- **Brain:** The drug enters the bloodstream, it then hits the brain which changes how you see, think, move and feel.

- **Nose:** Drugs can be sniffed, absorbed by the lining of the nose and dissolve straight into the bloodstream.

- **Mouth:** The drug is swallowed into the stomach, then enters the bloodstream. If smoked, the drug enters the lungs, then the bloodstream.

- **Veins:** The drug is injected straight into the bloodstream; fast acting.

- **Skin:** Some drugs can come in the form of tiny decorative transfers, which can be absorbed through the skin.

You wouldn't do some of those things to a dog.

Different drugs do different things to the body. They can make you feel relaxed, or full of energy and confidence, or even hallucinate. The important thing to realise is that these changes are unnatural and usually short lived. They can damage the body, especially if they're taken too often. A person who takes drugs is not in control of their body.

Why people use drugs

When people first take illegal drugs it's not because they need to take them, it's because they want to. There are many different reasons why people feel the need to use illegal drugs:

- **they think they can escape their problems**

- **they want to feel less stressed**

- **all their friends do it**

- **they like how drugs make them feel**

- **curiosity**

- **escape from physical/mental pain**

- **boredom**

Research has shown that there are three important factors in whether or not an individual will use drugs or not.

- **Parents:** Your parents can have an effect on this. Teenagers from unhappy homes are more likely to experiment with drugs. The values of your parents are also important. But, the biggest and most powerful influence is if your own parents take drugs. If they do, you're more likely to imitate them.

I'm lucky my parents were drug takers!

- **Friends:** Friends can be an important influence in encouraging
you to use drugs. Or you
may be a user and pick
friends who also take
drugs which can lead
to gang pressure.

- **Personality:** There isn't one personality 'type' that takes drugs, but one aspect of personality can predict non-drug use. People who follow the rules and values of their society are less likely. People who tend not to follow the crowd, and don't conform to rules are more likely to use drugs.

It's also been found that people who are impulsive, inconsiderate, untrustworthy, lacking in ambition with poor work habits are more likely to smoke, drink alcohol and take drugs. You probably know people who sound like this. They're also likely to start using them earlier.

Want some drugs, Baz?

> My life is pretty sheltered so it was a bit of a shock to find out someone I knew took drugs. She was a bit of a rebel and eventually was kicked out of school. I'm not sure what she's doing, now.
>
> (17-YEAR-OLD)

Cost

The trouble is, once you're into drugs it's a downward spiral. Because you develop a 'tolerance' you need more to get the same 'high' feeling. The more you take, the more you need and the more you want. It becomes a habit. An expensive habit! Because you reach the stage where you need the drug physically and mentally you may go to any lengths to get it.

Kicking the habit

Giving up is not easy and almost impossible to do alone. Drug users who want to kick the habit need support and help from their friends. Withdrawal brings with it unpleasant physical side effects like uncontrolled trembling, sweats, headaches and sickness. People who take drugs and want to give them up will find it very difficult. Helplines and clinics can help, but the biggest step a person doing drugs can take, is to want to give up. It's a choice between being in control or being controlled by an expensive habit.

Say 'no'

Sounds easy, doesn't it. But it isn't. Saying 'no' can be the hardest thing in the world if your friends are saying 'yes'! What you must remember is that drugs can kill, even the first time you try them. If they don't kill you, they can seriously damage your physical and mental health.

It's not always easy to tell if someone is on drugs until it's too late and they've become addicted. People know of the dangers and they know what is likely to happen to them. They know what trouble it can lead to as people drop out of school, become unsociable, unemployable, and thieve to maintain their habit. Adults can talk at you till they're blue in the face. You can watch television programmes telling you how some poor teenager died in a night-club after just one tab. But when all's said and done it's down to you. It's your decision as to what you put into your body and your own choice. Make the right one.

Other addictions

You will have heard the saying 'A little of what you fancy does you good' and 'Everything in moderation'. People who are looking for ways to escape reality and run away from their problems can turn to all sorts of different things. Sometimes they will get so focussed on that thing that they seem to find it their only comfort.

Gambling

People can get addicted to gambling, whether it's betting on horse racing, cards, lottery tickets, scratch cards, or playing machines down an arcade. Gambling is big business, and lots of people make lots of money out of the punters who take all the risk Most gamblers lose, most of the time. Few know when to stop. Gambling will not solve your problems, you will not get rich, you will waste your time and money. The odds are stacked against you heavily. The compulsion to win can be so strong that the need to find more money to bet can lead to theft and antisocial behaviour - like borrowing money and not paying it back, spending more and more time looking for a winner. But the winner never is just around the corner, on the next race, or on the next game or scratch card.

He's addicted to SCRATCH cards in a big way

Food

Have you ever felt really miserable and reached for a bar of chocolate? That's because chocolate contains a mood enhancer and gives you a lift, along with the sugar and salt content which may temporarily boost your energy. Some people however eat for comfort, and can't stop. They either seem to get addicted to one particular food, or they binge eat, eating massive amounts until they feel sick. If you get into a bad behaviour pattern of eating it's difficult to stop. You may put on weight and not like it. The you eat more because you feel miserable and you think the food will cheer you up, and anyway you deserve it, it's your reward and so it goes on. Food bingeing, and food control can lead to all sorts of problems and eating disorders, like anorexia, bulimia and obesity, particularly for people who feel their lives are out of control. If you have a problem, get help, there are plenty of people and organisations who can help you.

Sport

It's back to that moderation theme again! Any physical exercise which raises your heart rate and you exertion levels will lead to a point where the hormone endorphin will kick in. These are feel good hormones, and will give you that extra lift, or boost to continue your sport, game, marathon race, or run away from that angry bear Neanderthal man met in the Stone Ages. You may have noticed whilst exercising that there comes a moment just when you though you were flagging and maybe in pain, you suddenly find that extra strength from within. It may be determination to win at something, but it's more likely to be those endorphins.

There are usually two reasons why people get addicted to physical exercise. The first is to feel that good feeling again, and the second can lead from an obsession to have a perfect body. And it all goes back to people having low self-esteem, trying to find ways to improve their confidence, or to escape their stresses. Most people who are addicted to physical exercise don't realise that they are, until they start losing their friends as their obsession eats into their normal daily life.

Sometimes too much exercise is bad for you, especially if you are still growing: your bones, muscles and tendons will protest about the over use — by giving you lots of pain!

Risk-taking

Believe it or not, some people become addicted to taking risks! Like sport, taking a risk with something produces adrenaline. You feel 'high'. And if you are stressed, the risk may seem to reduce or remove the stress from your life.

Only it doesn't. Taking risks can be dangerous, especially if you do things like hanging out of train windows, holding onto trucks when roller-skating, dodging through traffic, walking through unsafe areas. The high that taking risks produces doesn't last. You will inevitably come down to earth with a large thud.

Where to get help

Just as there are millions of people, there are millions of things which people can become obsessed or addicted to in a way that interferes with their normal way of living: carrots, religion, chocolate, caffeine, sex, appearance, shopping, stealing, television soap series, going out, staying in, superstitions, medical problems, unsociable behaviour. You may know of some people with habits that are more than just eccentricities. But for every kind of addiction, there is someone else who has been through the same thing, and other people who can help you. So if you, or someone you know has a problem, what would you do to help yourself, or them?

CHAPTER 9

LOOK INTO MY EYES

The meaning of life

Many young people will find that they have already developed their own basic 'philosophy' of life. This means that you build up your own beliefs, attitudes, opinions and feelings about the world around you. You probably won't do this consciously, but you may suddenly find it difficult to accept the beliefs (or lack thereof) of adults around you. You may start to ask questions about the world or the very reason for living. Why am I here? Why did my parents have me? Why do bad things seem to happen to good people?

A greater power

Throughout the history of the world, many peoples and cultures have believed in something more than just a life on earth. Many people today believe in some greater divine power or powers who will look after them in some way and take a personal interest in their life. This can help people to feel more secure and it can also give them something to believe in, especially when things in life don't go that well. In a world where you feel little, perhaps taken for granted and unimportant compared to those around you, a protecting power that values you as an individual may seem very attractive. Belonging to a particular group of people can give you an identity. This is what religion gives to some people.

This doesn't necessarily mean that you have to accept or join a religious group or sect, but you may feel that you need a rigid religious framework to lean on, a group that you can belong to which has a clearly defined goal. A congregation can seem like a large uncritical extended family, and it's the actual sense of belonging somewhere and to something that becomes the main good feeling.

Material World

Others may take the opposite road and feel that any rigidly based religion would suffocate them and take away their individuality and freedom. Still others will take the view that religion is not for them at all. You may live on a level that is known as 'materialistic'. In other words you trust and believe in your own money and things you possess. Your destiny is really in your own hands and not in the hands of any greater being. Belief in a God or gods can be a very powerful and formative thing. Wars have been started, and are still being fought by people who cannot accept another's religion.

It's only in recent history that so many people have started to reject belief in any kind of supernatural power and religion. This could be because of education and the increased amount of scientific knowledge that we have as a society today. There's a danger here, though, that many children are growing up with nothing at all to hang onto.

The fact remains that some kind of spiritual background is very important for all of us. You must have something to believe in, even if it's your own self-worth. The lack of belief catches up even with those people who try to ignore it and will play a part, even if they don't realise it, in the way their feelings develop and emotional background.

The ink is black, the page is white

You may find that at this time in your life, you tend to see everything in black and white. Adult 'shades of grey' in between are not acceptable as a middle ground. If you think about it, thinking in this way is very safe. You may well believe in an absolute truth and an absolute wrong. It would be much simpler if this was the case. Unfortunately, you come to realise sooner or later, that it isn't! Arguments may arise between you and adults because of this different outlook on important issues. Adults will tend to judge things on their merits and take other (unimportant, or so you think) factors into account before making a judgement.

Only adults can see shades of grey!

Religion

Is it better if you've been brought up with a definite religious teaching, or not? Each view has its 'fors' and 'againsts'.

The advantages of religious teaching are that:

- **The religious group may have given you help, support, and a sense of belonging;**
- **It could also have given you a good guidance in positive and social ways of behaving.**
- **It gives you a relationship with God**

The advantages of not having religious teaching are that:

- **You can start afresh and form your own opinions about things;**
- **Your views will be your own and won't be biased or affected by anyone else;**
- **You can choose your own religion rather than being born into a particular family faith.**

If you come from a strongly religious home you may feel that you want to break away when you become an adolescent to become agnostic (someone who believes that it's impossible to know if God exists) or atheistic (someone who thinks that there isn't a God) or to choose a different faith and religion from those around you.

You won't take kindly to people telling you what you ought to do during this time. This is another 'phase' that you have to work through, and you'll probably come out of it a wiser and better person, but your beliefs about the world and religion are personal and something that you must sort out for yourself.

Religion and obsession

You may also know someone who takes the opposite road and develops a deep obsession with religion in one form or another. If this happens to you or to one of your friends then the best advice to give is to stand back, just for a little while to be really sure of the path they want to take. Don't go anywhere you're not absolutely sure of, or that you've a feeling you may regret later. If you feel you are being pressured by people into a pattern of thinking you are not sure of, then ask advice from someone who is objective and knowledgeable. Someone like a Religious Education teacher at school or college may have a knowledge of most kinds of religion, or will know where to find out more. There are some 'churches' or 'sects' who do not take a normal or moderate view of life and religion. Some of these people are on a mission to recruit others, and can be very persuasive that their way is right. There are some fanatical faiths who will particularly prey on the weak, lonely or stressed. If you are unsure about people like this you may meet, check it out with someone who knows.

Belief and stress

Without any spiritual belief, religious or otherwise, a person has no basic source of hope, comfort or courage. If you have nothing in your life to believe in, you destroy any faith you have (not just religious, but for example, faith and trust in people). This will do your stress levels no good at all, because by isolating yourself and making yourself an island, you can't hope to solve any problems, you only leave yourself alone with them. We all need other people whether we like to admit that or not, and we all need to believe in a future in this life, as well as perhaps, beyond.

A belief in God, whether as an outside influence, or within yourself can give you something to talk and pray to when the going gets tough. Many of the well known religions have churches which are happy spiritual centres of a community, who provide all sorts of meeting groups, events, friends and support, especially in times of crisis. If you feel lost, religion can give you direction and hope, but beware any group who try to change your way of thinking, take you away from friends and family, take control of your money, or leave you feeling bad or guilty.

Things that go bump in the night

Sometimes when people are in trouble, they will turn to anything which might give them hope, no matter how much it costs. Once again, these may be people who have not really looked hard at themselves to see if they can find their own solutions.

Look at yourself to see if you can find a solution!

expensive ways

Reading your astrological horoscope in a magazine is one thing, and indeed, they may sometimes be amazingly accurate. But horoscopes are often a matter of how you interpret them, and are usually pretty vague so could seem true for a lot of people. Horoscopes can be seen as a kind of fortune telling, and there are lots of other methods people may claim to be accurate.

- **Palm reading** - where it's believed that each of the lines on your hand can tell the story of your life.

- **Tea leaf or other readings** - where the shapes formed are meant to have significant meanings.

- **Tarot cards** - which are an ancient form of prediction with different cards representing different situations and people.

- **Reading people's auras or energies** - some people say they can see colours or shapes around peoples bodies.

- **Crystal ball gazing** - where the reader can see shapes and events through gazing into the glass, Dowsing - using twigs or rods to find water, metals or elements beneath the ground, or watching the pendulum swing of, for

example, a crystal dangling on a thread which may say 'Yes' or 'No' to a question.

- **Psychics** - who believe they can receive messages from dead spirits.

- **Numerology** - where numbers like birth dates or letters of a name may have supposed significant meanings.

- And dozens of new and bizarre ideas people come up with every week. Some fortune tellers seem to have a real ability, and are uncannily accurate, others are simply thieves and charlatans who tell you what they think you want to hear whilst charging

into a situation where you won't make a decision unless you've thrown a dice, or read a horoscope you are on dangerous ground. Fortune telling can become compulsive and addictive in much the way that superstitions can, particularly to people in times of trouble.

Are there any superstitions you or your family have? Do they make you laugh, or do you take them seriously? The funny thing is that people from different countries have entirely different superstitions and symbols for luck. The number 13 may be seen as unlucky in the UK, but terribly lucky in Italy. A black cat is good news if it crosses the path of an English person, and seriously bad news if it happens to a Russian!

You must make your own decisions and your own judgements, a palm reader cannot do that for you. It is harmless enough to not walk under a ladder, or salute a solo magpie, but if you find yourself avoiding every crack in the pavement or touching every piece of wood you find for luck, you have problem. If you have a difficult decision to make, or think a psychic can tell you that a lottery win is due next Wednesday, they can't. Life is not about luck, it's not totally predictable, it's about being in a certain place at a certain time and certain things occurring. It's how you deal with those events, stresses and problems which matter, not about whether your horoscope said you'd have a bad day and the number eight would be lucky for some!

Cracks in the pavement - unlucky?

No sweat!

CHAPTER 10

STRESSBUSTERS

What you gonna do?

This book has given you lots of ideas about how stress can affect you, and some of the problems which could result. But knowledge can be power, and by knowing and recognising some of the problems which can result when people are under pressure and stress, you can work out ways to solve them. Once you realise how stressed out life has made you, you then have to think of ways to relieve the stress you are feeling. This is different for different people. Some of us relax by playing sport, others of us like to hang out with a few friends and talk about nothing in particular.

Whatever works for you. The simple fact is that all of us need 'time out' occasionally to get our heads back together, or to calm down. There are two main ways that you do this.

Stress relief!

Problem-focused stressbusting

One way to reduce stress is to deal with the cause of it. This is known as a problem-focused strategy. So you may:

- Try to get to the root of the problem first and then make a list of potential solutions. Discuss these with a friend or advisor.

- Remove or avoid whatever it is that's stressing you out.

- Take some control of the stress. (For example you may start to plan your time better.) If you feel you have no control over the problem it will make your stress worse.

- Change yourself inside — change your outlook on life. Perhaps unrealistic goals are causing stress?

Emotion-focused stressbusting

The second main way you may try and deal with your stress is by tackling and trying to reduce the negative emotions that are involved. So you may:

- Start some relaxation therapy, such as listening to music, meditation, yoga, massage, or even taking a nice warm bath.

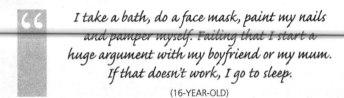

I take a bath, do a face mask, paint my nails and pamper myself. Failing that I start a huge argument with my boyfriend or my mum. If that doesn't work, I go to sleep.

(16-YEAR-OLD)

- Use what is known as biofeedback. This is where you try to control your heart rate when you know something has stressed you out. Some people use monitors (which measure pulse rate, blood pressure, or even how much moisture is present on the skin) to help them do this. The idea is that you relax until your body is back to normal.

- Be more assertive and take control of the situation.

- Exercise, get rid of your anger in a safe way, or find support from close friends.

- Find some way to distract yourself, for some this could even mean tidying your room! (Yeah, really!)

 I chill out by eating loads, especially chocolate to treat myself. I also either listen to music or watch one of my favourite videos.
(17-YEAR-OLD)

- If your stress becomes very difficult for you to control then your doctor may prescribe drug therapy using anti-anxiety medication. Obviously the problem here is not to let the person become physically or mentally dependent on them.

Other ways to chill

Some other ways to chill, from 16 and 17-year-olds:

- **watch soppy films**
- **throw things up the wall, like pens**
- **watch 'Titanic' and get involved**
- **sing to loud music watch television**
- **play football or any sport**
- **go out with my mates**

- **ride my bike**
- **eat chocolate**
- **slam doors**
- **scream**
- **read**
- **kiss my girlfriend**

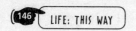
• cry a lot (it makes me feel better)   • shout—it always works

• vacuum anywhere with a vengeance   • pluck my eyebrows

• set myself goals or targets   • pick my zits

• cuddling or looking after pets   • watching my goldfish

• Staring at my lava lamp and thinking nothing

• aromatherapy oils, joss sticks and any nice smells

You are not alone

The worst thing you can do in times of stress is try to deal with the problem all by yourself. All that happens is that your thoughts and worries start to tie themselves in knots, and become a vicious circle of worry and confusion. Lying awake at night thinking about what tomorrow might bring will not change anything. You'll just be more tired and miserable by the morning.

You may be suffering from a situation which is not of your making, so it's not a case of a problem you can solve because it's outside events which are giving you grief. This is when it's most important to share your load with someone else. It's good to talk to close friends and people you trust who will support you with a listening ear and a cuddle, who will let you cry if you need to, or get mad with frustration. But friends don't always have an answer about the way forward - your worries may be too big for them to deal with. This is where the advice of an outsider may come in useful. There are lots of trained experts out there who can handle all sorts of problems. They will listen calmly and objectively, and because they are not emotionally involved in your worries may be able to give you ideas and advice that you and your friends may not have thought of. There are counsellors, school counsellors, youth workers, social workers, psychologists, educational psychologists, psychiatrists, priests, doctors, and a whole number of organisations trained to help you.

You must ask for help, or get someone to ask for you. Starting points are through a trusted teacher at school, your doctor, telephone advice lines, the internet, social services, or your local Citizens Advice Bureau. Remember, you have absolutely nothing to lose by asking these professionals for help for yourself, or on behalf of a friend.

Who you gonna call?

If you ever feel completely desperate and alone, and you really believe there is no one you can talk to their are telephone advice lines open 24 hours a day you can contact, such as Childline, or the Samaritans. A telephone operator will put you through to many of these services free of charge, so you don't even have to have money in your pocket. Telephone operators are trained to do this, and will not ask any questions of you. The people at the end of the telephone helplines will not ask your name or your address if you choose not to give it to them, they are completely confidential, and will make no judgements about how you feel or what you want to tell them.

In other frightening or dangerous situations, ask for help, find people, shops, pubs, an adult woman, a house with a light on, a passing car, a telephone box. If you think you are being followed, or someone is bothering you, trust your instinct, run, scream, go somewhere where there are other people. But firstly, use your personal safety common sense to not get you into risky situations.

Taking time out

If your problems are home based, maybe you will need a change of scene at some point. if it's a family issue, maybe you could suggest that the whole family takes some time out. Perhaps a short holiday is possible just to give everyone a break. This could be for you all, your parents, or just for yourself. Why not get the family together in one place and have a discussion or brainstorming session about what may be possible. If the problem involves a sick member of the family, it may be possible for that person to get some respite care in a home or hospital just to give you all a breather. Your family or medical social worker will be able to help here.

Maybe you need a rest. Is it possible for you to stay with a friend for a weekend? Or if you need a completely different environment, is there a family friend or relative you could go to for a short break?

If things are so stressful at home that you are in danger of being thrown out, or are considering running away contact your social services. It may be that short term fostering with a local family (so that you can stay at the same school or job and around friends), a placement in a children's or young persons' home, or supported lodgings may be available. The last thing anyone wants to happen is for you to be homeless and hanging around. Living on the streets is not better than living somewhere with a bed, food and warmth however attractive the idea may seem at times. It is also a difficult trap to get out of.

Chilling out

Relaxation is the key to keeping calm, and helping your stressed out brain staying unscrambled. You will have your own ways of relaxing — listening to music — reading — writing down your feelings in a diary — watching television — sport — dancing — hobbies and dozens of others. If you are ever stuck for new ideas try looking at your school, library, community, youth club or church notice boards for ideas of different things you could join or try.

Also check out local groups and further education centres for methods which teach relaxation through classes. Some of the most successful are yoga, tai chi and meditation classes, but there are lots of others. Here you will be taught to completely focus you mind, body and breathing to the exclusion of every other problem you may have. This temporary respite, even if only for an hour's class will give your whole brain and body a break. It will also teach you how to relax using the same methods for yourself at home.

Getting to sleep

Many people have trouble sleeping when they are worried. Their brains are so active with thinking about the past and the future that they don't seem to want to stop and relax enough for you to get to sleep. Then you might find yourself dreaming your worries, and waking up frequently. This lack of sleep will only add to your problems. A tired brain and body can't function properly. Your reactions will slow, your concentration will be poor, your stresses will seem greater, and you may get aches and pains and spots.

Try all the obvious methods first:

Bad idea, drinking it all

• Don't drink anything containing caffeine (tea, coffee, coke, alcohol etc) after 6pm each evening.

• Don't eat junk food containing lots of 'e' numbers; caffeine and many 'e' numbers are all stimulants and will wake you up.

mmm, maybe not?

• Make sure you are not hungry. Better to eat a good meal earlier in the evening though, than a huge doorstep sandwich last thing at night which your body has not had time to digest before you lie down.

• Try warm milk, camomile tea, or any of the over-the-chemists' counter calming herb or vitamin preparations, which are safe if taken according to the instructions. If you are already on medication for a medical problem, check out with your chemist or doctor before taking some of the supplements like St John's Wort.

- Don't do anything too exciting just before bedtime. A horror story book or video may leave you wide awake. Better to watch a calmer film, or read a quieter kind of book or magazine. Reading something positive, like a good novel, will relax you. Your eyes will get tired and so want to close, and the subject matter will distract you from your worries.

I shouldn't watch horror vids last thing at night!

It's your bedtime!

- Don't go to bed too late, nor get up too late. If you consistently change your bedtime hours you'll almost give yourself a kind of jet lag, which will make it difficult to get up when you need to. This is particularly true following weekends. If you've changed your sleep times by several hours, no wonder it's so difficult to get up on a Monday morning! Most young people need 8 to 10 hours sleep every night to stay fit and well.

- Take a relaxing bath — not too hot, as that can wake you up. Try some tranquil aromatherapy oils, eg. Lavender oil.

- Listen to music, but again of the quieter variety, not the sort which makes you want to get out of bed and dance!

aaah!

- Try visualisation, meditation or relaxation. There are lots of tapes and books which will teach you relaxation methods ranging from visualisation to self hypnosis. These are excellent to try or to listen to at bedtime. They work by getting you to focus on your breathing — to slow it down and calm you, to relax the muscles of your body — so that you let go of all the days tension, and to visualise something pleasant — which will focus your mind and stop your brain hassling away at you about your stresses. Tense and relax each of your muscles in turn, starting from your feet and working all the way up to your head. Feel more relaxed with each set of muscles you relax.

Visualisation techniques

Make sure you are comfortable, not too hot and not too cold if possible. Turn off your bedroom lights and try to have the room as dark as you like it. Get into your cosy sleeping position and close your eyes. Ignore any outside noises, they are not relevant. Now start using your imagination to picture a nice scene. Lots of people like to imagine a beach scene. They visualise that they are on a nice warm beach, listening to the sounds of the waves lapping at the shore, feeling the warm sun on their body, no-one and nothing else around to disturb them. And that's all you need to do. Keep seeing that scene, and feeling those good and happy comfortable feelings. other people use a scene where they are walking down some steps towards a favourite place. This could be a garden you know, or somewhere with very happy memories. If you can't think of a place, create a scene you know would make you really happy. Keep walking down those steps towards that nice place, feeling more relaxed and calm with every step. Another idea is to imagine a leaf in the centre of a pond, walk into the warm water of that beautiful place and start floating and swimming towards that leaf. Keep focussed on your goal. If a noise, or an itch disturbs you, just bring your focus back to your happy place and carry on calmly.

Because these visualisations focus your mind, it distracts you from the worries which are keeping you awake. At the very least it will calm you and give you some inner peace. Most people find they can make visualisation work so well — and it can take a little practice — that they are asleep before they reach the leaf in the pond, or the place at the bottom of the steps!

Medicine

If all else fails, and lack of sleep is making you ill and wretched it's time to go to your doctor who may prescribe sleeping, calming or mood enhancing medication for you. There are some very good medicines these days which are not addictive, nor do they make you sleepy during the day. You are not a failure if you need to take medicine; some of the strongest, most together people have had times where they have needed outside help to get them through a bad patch in their lives. Help is there. All you need to do is ask. It's a sign of strength if you ask for help!

Complementary medicine

A little research in your local or school library will tell you a lot about some of the following, and you can judge whether they might work for you. Complementary medicine should be seen as exactly that, complementary, and not as an alternative to usual treatments or medicines which you might need for a medical problem. One of the most successful, and one which is now recognised by the authorities and sometimes available via your doctor is Acupuncture. Very fine needles will be inserted at energy lines on your body which have been determined by years of practice and knowledge which originated in ancient China. These needles will stimulate your energies and help your mind and body to heal itself. They do not hurt!

There are lots of other both traditional and new treatments which work very successfully to de-stress many people such as massage, homeopathy, hypnotherapy, accupressure, aromatherapy massage, and osteopathy. Some of these are available via you doctor, many need to be paid for. Having read up on them, you might want to give them a try. First ask around for personal recommendation. Next try your telephone directory or organisations which many qualified practitioners of these treatments will belong to, to find someone in your area. If you are unsure of a practitioner, always take someone with you and keep them in the same room during your treatment. There are quacks out there who have come up with some bizarre ideas of how to de-stress you, whilst charging an awful lot of money. If you think walking across a bed of burning coals, or lying on a bed of needles will add to your stress, don't do it, and don't waste your time and especially your or someone else's money!

Knowledge is power

There is masses of information out there waiting for you to pick it up. Whatever your problem stress or issues there is probably a leaflet, an organisation, a tape, a video, or a book on it. Books may take the form of non-fiction — like this one — which provide information, or they may be fiction, where a story revolves around an issue which might be relevant to you. If you think you could learn more about how to deal with your stresses or worries, then try a book that's appropriate for you. Most of these will be books written for adults, many come under the theme of self-help. A lot of them are written so clearly that you will be able to understand the bits which could help you.

Many of these books teach you how to feel more positive, how to change your negative thought patterns, and how to tackle problems you are faced with. If you practise some of the methods they suggest, you may find a whole new, more confident positive person will emerge from the bad space you are in. There are lots of great books for young adults, many are humourous, but most deal with the major worries of many teenagers such as parents, love, sex, drugs and your body. If you want something more specific, then you will need the Self Help, the Psychology, the Medicine, or the Education sections of your library, book shop or the Internet bookselling web sites to locate the titles right for you. Don't be afraid to ask a bookseller or a librarian if there is a book for your particular worry, they've heard them all.. On the self help side there are some

great titles such as When I say no I feel guilty, I'm OK You're OK and If It Hurts It Isn't Love which immediately give you an idea of what they are about. Read the back cover, and a couple of pages to see if it's for you, and whether you can make sense of the text. Some titles may be from overseas and a little difficult to understand, others may be aimed at university students and academics and could be tough for you to follow without some previous background knowledge of the subject.

Knowledge is power, and the more information you have about a problem, the more able you will be to deal with it. Knowing how to help yourself or a friend keep emotionally healthy, is every bit as important as looking after your body. Everyone will get stressed at some point in their lives, but you can get through it, and you are not alone. Don't suffer in silence, don't look back, think about today and tomorrow and how you can make it better for yourself. Bust that stress!

Who you gonna call? STRESSBUSTERS!

APPENDIX

Useful Contacts (UK)

Some Basic Info

Remember, your school, local library, Citizens Advice Bureau, Borough and County Council, Social Services, health centre, and local telephone directories (check under health and welfare services, emergency helplines, and young peoples organisations) will all have contact numbers and addresses for every kind of organisation, helpline or charity you may need.

Some of the helplines are manned by trained counsellors, some are trained volunteers. Whatever you want to ask or to say, they will know how to help you, and many of the issues people ask, have been asked many times before.

Offering support, counselling, referral to other organisations and advice many of the helplines have Freephone numbers. Some of the Freephone helpline numbers will not appear on a telephone bill; these tend to be the 0800 numbers. This means you could make a call, and no-one will know. Ask the helpline when you call.

Some of the helplines can be very busy, and some are open at restricted times only, in which case you will hear an answerphone message with the details of when you can call. Don't give up, keep trying, you will get through. It may be useful to have a pen and paper handy. Sometimes the numbers change, and you will need to write another one down. You may also be referred to another organisation or group, perhaps one near you. You do not have to give your name or address if you don't want to, the person answering the helpline will just refer to you as 'Caller'. Calls are

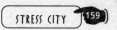

treated in strictest confidence. Here are just a few of the numbers available:

- **Alateen** part of **Al-Anon**, for young people affected by drink problems, whether themselves, or someone close: Lines open 10am–5pm Mon–Fri, answering machine with contact numbers after hours: ☎ **020 7403 0888**
  🌐 **www.al-anon-alateen.org**

- **Childline** a helpline for all kinds of problems children may experience, including abuse and being at risk: ☎ **0800 1111**
  🌐 **www.childline.org.uk**

- **CRUSE** for advice and support with bereavement following a death. Hours open between mid-afternoon and mid-evening: ☎ **0345 585565** or check local telephone directory.

- **Families Anonymous** for help with friends and families with drug problems. Hours 1–4pm Mon–Fri, answering machine with contact numbers or to leave a message: ☎ **020 7498 4680**

- **LIFE** for counselling and help with all kinds of issues surrounding pregnancy, and abortion. Answering machine in the evening: ☎ **01926 311511** and ☎ **020 7825 2500** for enquiries 9am to 5pm

- **NSPCC** the National Society for the Prevention of Cruelty to Children: ☎ **0800 800500** 🌐 **www.nspcc.org.uk**

- **Samaritans** help for those in despair or feeling suicidal: ☎ **0345 909090** if you can't remember this number and need it in an emergency, just dial **100** and ask the operator to put you through to the Samaritans.
  🌐 **www.samaritans.org.uk**

- **Saneline** for support, advice and information to do with all kinds of mental health problems, whether for yourself, or another person you are close to. Hours 12 noon–2pm: ☎ **0345 678000**

- **Sexwise** a helpline for teenagers with questions and issues surrounding sex, emergency contraception and sexuality (hetrosexual and homosexual). Hours 7am–midnight every day. ☎ **0800 282930** This number will not appear on a bill payers telephone bill.

- **Shelterline** for help with homelessness and housing problems: ☎ **0808 8004444** 🌐 **www.shelter.org.uk** not a helpline

- **Terence Higgins Trust** for information and advice about HIV and AIDS. Lines open 24 hours: ☎ **0800 567123 (National Aids Helpline)** also helpline 12 noon–10pm daily on: ☎ **020 7242 1010** 🌐 **www.tht.org.uk**

- **Youth Access** a national organisation for young people for advice and counselling. Hours 9am–1pm, 2pm–5pm. Answering machine outside office hours: ☎ **0208 772 9900**

- **Friend** for people unsure about their sexuality or wanting to talk about their feelings of homosexuality, lesbianism or bisexuality. Offers advice and counselling. Also available for parents. Local counselling groups too. ☎ **020 7837 3337** 7.30pm–10pm everday

Many of these organisations will have local numbers and support groups near you, see your local telephone directory.

🌐 **Note: for privacy you can use internet cafes, addresses in local telephone directory. Alternatively, local libraries often have computers linked up to the web.**